Grieve Well
to
Live Well

Finding Hope, Healing, and
Purpose Beyond Loss

David McBroom

Copyedited by Sam Severn
Interior design and layout by Rachel L. Hall, Writely Divided Editing & More

Grieve Well to Live Well: Finding Hope, Healing, and Purpose Beyond Loss / David McBroom. –1st edition.

ISBN: 979-8-9988993-0-0 Softcover
979-8-9988993-1-7 Hardcover
979-8-9988993-2-4 eBook

For Cathy - My Forever Love

You were my greatest love, my greatest joy, and my greatest blessing.
This book is a tribute to the life we shared, the love that endures,
and the faith that carries me forward.

Contents

CHAPTER 3

CHAPTER 4

CHAPTER 5

CHAPTER 6

Finding Healing Through Serving 81

CHAPTER 7

Faith and Grief – Wrestling with God 95

CHAPTER 8

Hope Beyond the Horizon 109

CHAPTER 9

CHAPTER 10

Foreword

MANY YEARS AGO, it was suggested to me that the more acquainted I was with a book's author, the more apt I would be to pick up their book and engage with its contents. The suggestion was offered with specific reference to one's love for the Scriptures. The idea was that my love for the Bible would be enhanced as I became more acquainted with its author, the Holy Spirit. It was good advice, and the level of my engagement with God's Word over time is probably a mirrored reflection of the depth of my relationship and intimacy with the Holy Spirit at any given time.

The concept certainly relates directly to a person's interest in the Bible, but I have also found it to be generally true. When I know an author, the more eager and receptive I am to read what they write and to hear what they have to say. When I know an author, I approach their work with eagerness, openness, and trust, all of which are born out of relationship.

I know the author of this book. My relationship with Dave and Cathy McBroom spans the better part of thirty years, and it has been a mutual blessing. We have walked together, dreamed together, ministered together, shared meals together, laughed together, and cried together. Then, when Dave lost Cathy from this earthly life, and she made her eternal entrance to heaven, we sorrowed together.

So, when Dave presented me with the first couple of chapters from the manuscript of his book, I eagerly received and devoured them because I know the author. I immediately followed up with a request for the full manuscript, and Dave was generous to share it with me. My relationship with Dave was a warm invitation to consume more of his writing, and because I know the author, I was fully engaged. As I followed Dave's reflections on loss and the accompanying grief journey, I did so with full assurance that what I read was honest, sincere, and full of integrity because I know the author.

If you do not know Dave McBroom, I invite you to become better acquainted with him through this volume. His transparent sharing provides intimate insight into him as a person and into the depth of his grief journey. Dave's real-life experience and scriptural knowledge provide a valuable backdrop for the practical lessons he learned on the difficult and sometimes lonely path of grief he traveled. Not only will you benefit from learning more about the author, but the insights Dave shares about navigating the loss of his dear wife, Cathy, will inform and encourage you in your own experience, if not now, then for the future.

In my current role as a pastoral counselor, I readily recognized that the Lord guided Dave as he told his story and forwarded the valuable lessons he learned. Scriptural truth came to life for Dave as he experienced the life-giving nature of passages like Psalm 34:18 (NIV) in real-time, "The LORD is close to the brokenhearted and saves those who are crushed in spirit." The Holy Spirit drew alongside Dave as he traversed an arduous journey of loss and sorrow, fulfilling the promise of Jesus from Matthew 5:4, "Blessed are those who mourn, for they will be comforted."

I invite you to become acquainted with my friend and colleague, Dave McBroom, and his writings. I am confident you will not be disappointed because I know this author.

In *agape*,

Reverend Les Welk
Pastoral counselor, colleague and friend of the author

Introduction

An Invitation to Walk Together

GRIEF IS SOMETHING NO ONE TRULY UNDERSTANDS until they walk through it themselves. Before losing my wife Cathy, I had ministered to grieving families, officiated funerals, and offered comfort to those experiencing loss. But when my own world was shattered, when I stood at the edge of an empty future I never imagined, I realized something – nothing can fully prepare you for the weight of grief.

I remember searching for answers, for guidance, for anything that could help me make sense of the pain. Some days, I didn't even know what I was looking for – I just knew I didn't want to feel alone in it. If you've picked up this book, maybe you feel the same way. If so, I want you to know this book is for you. This book exists because grief is a journey no one should have to walk alone.

The Three-Fold Purpose of this Book

I wrote this book for three reasons:

1. **To share my story and journey through grief.** This is the most personal thing I've ever written. I want to share the raw, unfiltered journey of what grief looked like for me – not just the pain, but the choices I made to grieve well so I could live well. My hope is that, in reading my story, you will find pieces of your own story reflected in these pages.

2. **To leave a legacy for my children and grandchildren.** Family has always been at the center of my life. Cathy and I built a legacy together, and I want my children, grandchildren, and even great-grandchildren to know the story of how we loved, how we grieved, and how we found hope beyond loss. I want them to see that grief does not define a life – love and purpose do.

3. **To help as many people as possible through their journey of grief.** When I was in the depths of grief, I desperately needed someone to tell me, "You're going to be okay. It won't always feel like this." I want to be that voice for you. My prayer is that this book will serve as a guide, a companion, and a source of hope for anyone navigating the road of loss. You are not alone.

What You'll Find in These Pages

This book is not just about grief – it's about what comes after. It's about what it means to grieve well so that you can live well. Grief is a journey no one should have to walk alone.

You'll find:

- **Moments of deep honesty** – because grief is messy, unpredictable, and real.

- **Lessons I learned along the way** – from Scriptures, from my family, from grief books, and from simply living through it.

- **Encouragement to keep going** – because even in the darkest moments, hope is waiting.

- **Study guides** – designed to help you reflect, process, and find healing – whether you work through them on your own or in a small group.

At the end of each chapter, you'll find a brief summary of the key themes, along with reflection and discussion questions to help you apply what you've read. There is space provided for journaling and personal responses.

There is no right way to grieve and no set timeline for healing. Go at your own pace. Some chapters may resonate more deeply than others. Some questions may stir emotions you weren't expecting. That's okay. This isn't a checklist – it's a companion for your journey.

Wherever you are in your journey, I want you to know this:

You are not alone. Hope is real.
And your story is far from over.

This book is not a quick fix. It won't erase the pain of loss. But I believe with all my heart that if you are willing to do the work of grieving well, you will find life again.

If you're holding this book in your hands, I already know something about you: You are searching for hope. I want to tell you: Hope is real. Joy is possible. And though grief will change you, it does not have to destroy you.

This is my story. My journey. But more than that, this is an invitation:

- An invitation to **grieve well.**

- An invitation to **live well.**

- An invitation to **step forward into a life where hope still exists beyond the horizon of loss.**

Let's walk this journey together.

Grieve Well
to
Live Well

Shattered Dreams
and Unexpected Paths

The Excitement of New Beginnings - Packing Up and Moving On

THE HOUSE WAS FULL OF BOXES, BUT NOT JUST ANY BOXES – these were filled with 33 years of memories. After more than three decades in the same home, Cathy and I were ready for something new.

We weren't just moving; we were having our first-ever custom home built. It was something we had dreamed about for years, but now it was finally happening. Our old house had served us well, but it was small – barely 1700 square feet. The kitchen was tiny, barely big enough for two people to squeeze in without bumping elbows. Cathy always laughed about how we mastered the art of navigating that little space, but we both dreamed of more room to breathe, to gather, and to host our growing family.

The new home was going to be everything we had worked and saved for. The kitchen alone was bigger than anything we had ever had, with a nine-foot island stretching across the center. Cathy was especially excited. She talked about all the family gatherings we'd host, the meals she'd cook, and the memories we'd make in that space. She was looking forward to every corner of that house, imagining the fresh start it represented.

We could almost see our future unfolding there – lazy mornings with coffee in that spacious kitchen, holidays filled with laughter echoing off the walls that had never known anyone's story but ours.

We imagined the joy of having our grandkids over, their laughter echoing as they played in the ping-pong room we had set up just for them. The new house wasn't just about square footage or upgraded appliances – it was about what it represented. It was the culmination of decades of dreams, sacrifice, and steady faithfulness. We had poured our lives into ministry, into raising our children, into serving others. This home felt like a quiet reward – a place where we could finally slow down, breathe deep, and savor the life we had built together.

For Cathy, it was a place of rest after years of giving so much to others. For me, it was a chance to watch her flourish in a space she had long imagined. Every design choice, every piece of furniture we picked out, every conversation about where to hang the pictures or what color to paint the walls – it all carried *meaning*. It wasn't just a house: It was a promise of time together. A place to grow old. A sacred place to laugh, love, and live.

That's why what came next was so devastating. The home we thought would mark a new beginning became a place of unexpected endings. And yet, even in that, God was present – though His presence looked different than I had hoped.

What we didn't know was that, despite all the excitement and anticipation, Cathy would never get to fully enjoy that home. Life had a different plan – and though I couldn't see it then, God also had a different plan. At the time it didn't feel like a plan at all. It felt like everything we had dreamed of was slipping through our fingers. But this was only the beginning of a journey that I never expected to take – one that would test my faith, my strength, and everything I thought I knew about hope.

A Subtle Shift Before the Storm

In the middle of packing boxes and planning for our new life, Cathy started experiencing these little moments where she couldn't quite get the words out. It wasn't dramatic – no sudden pain, no alarming collapse – just a hesitation, as if her mind was moving faster than her mouth could keep up.

We laughed it off at first. After all, we were both tired from packing, juggling family events, and all the excitement of the move. Maybe it was just stress or exhaustion. But something about it didn't sit right with me. Then, for the first time in over 50 years of marriage, Cathy looked at me and said, "I think you need to take me to the emergency room."

The words stunned me. Cathy was strong, always brushing off little aches and pains, never one to overreact. But hearing her say that? It was like a switch flipped inside of me. That quiet, uneasy feeling I'd been pushing aside suddenly grew louder. Still, I told myself it was probably nothing serious.

It was Friday – the day of my granddaughter Ashley's wedding rehearsal. We were supposed to be getting ready for a night of celebration, but instead we found ourselves in a sterile ER, waiting for answers.

At the ER, the doctors moved quickly. A CT scan showed fluid, not in her lungs like we first assumed, but in her chest cavity. I tried to stay calm, but inside, everything felt upside down. It was one of those moments where nothing made sense, and all I could do was lean into what I knew to be true: *"Trust in the LORD with all your heart and lean not on your own understanding; in all your ways acknowledge Him, and He shall direct your paths"* (Proverbs 3:5–6). I didn't understand what was happening – but I chose to trust that God was still leading us, even through this.

The doctor's face stayed calm, but I could sense the shift in his tone. He decided to do a biopsy, drawing a sample of the fluid to send off for further testing. We sat there, waiting in that sterile, too-quiet room, the hum of machines filling the silence between us. I kept telling myself it was probably pneumonia or something simple. Still, the sight of Cathy hooked up to monitors, waiting for answers, felt heavier than I wanted to admit. Even as I tried to stay strong for her, a quiet ache was growing inside me – a sense that life as we knew it was starting to change. I silently clung to what I had always believed: *"And we know that all things work together for good to those who love God, to those who are the called according to His purpose"* (Romans 8:28). I had preached this verse, quoted it to others in their pain, but now I was the one needing to believe it – when everything felt so uncertain. And the truth is, I couldn't see anything good in that moment.

Choosing Joy Amidst Uncertainty

Later that day, Cathy was released. We returned home. Despite everything we had just heard at the hospital, Cathy didn't hesitate: "We're going to that rehearsal," she said, with a determined smile. That was Cathy, always choosing joy, always showing up for the people she loved. And honestly, I wanted to believe everything was still okay. I clung to the hope that the test was just a precaution, that we'd get answers soon, and they'd tell us it was nothing serious. So we went. That Friday night, surrounded by family and friends, it felt like we had stepped into a different world – one without hospitals or X-rays, where life felt simple and joyful again.

Watching my granddaughter Ashley rehearse her vows, seeing Cathy smile at her from her chair out on the lawn, I let myself believe, even if just for a little while, that everything would be fine.

The next day – Saturday – was nothing short of magical. I had the honor of officiating Ashley's wedding, standing at the front as she began a new chapter of her life. The wedding was held outdoors on Camano Island, with a stunning view of the Puget Sound water, and a landscape that looked like it had been painted by God Himself. It was the most beautiful setting I'd ever performed a wedding in – absolutely idyllic. Cathy sat in the front row, her eyes sparkling with pride and love, soaking in every moment.

After the ceremony, we laughed, we danced, and for those few precious hours, the weight of the unknown disappeared. Cathy was radiant, moving with ease, her laughter echoing through the open air. I remember thinking, *She's fine. This is just a scare; we'll get through it.* Looking back, I'm grateful we had that day – the gift of joy before everything changed.

The Diagnosis - When Everything Changed

After the wedding, life felt like it was holding its breath – like the calm before a storm you don't yet know is coming. We had sold our home, but our new one wasn't ready yet. To take our minds off everything, we went on a four-day vacation to Lake Chelan – just the two of us. It was a much-needed escape, and a generous gift from our pastor, Troy Jones, who graciously offered us his home there for free. We gladly accepted, hoping that a few days away would give us the space to breathe, reflect, and simply be together.

After that, we stayed with our children, grateful for the familiar comfort of family while we waited. We tried to hold onto the joy of Ashley's wedding, soaking in the beauty of those days – but beneath it all was a quiet tension. We were both waiting for answers we didn't want to hear. While we were staying with our children, we met with the Oncologist at the Seattle Cancer Care Alliance hospital. We had made the appointment, hoping for clarity, maybe even some good news – a sliver of hope we could hold on to. But nothing could have prepared us for what the Oncologist said.

His words were steady, but final. "It's Stage IV Ovarian cancer," he told us. Then came the words that will forever echo in my mind: "I'm afraid there's no cure, no hope." In that moment, my heart shattered. The weight of it pressed so heavily on us both that I could hardly breathe. And yet, somewhere deep in that silence, a truth whispered its way into my soul: *"The LORD is near to those who have a broken heart and saves those who have a contrite spirit"* (Psalm 34:18). I didn't know how we'd face the days ahead, but I knew God was close.

Our youngest daughter, Jamie, was in the office with us, sitting quietly by Cathy's side. I remember glancing at her as the words hung heavy in the air – her face pale, her eyes wide with disbelief. We had our other daughter, Heidi, on the speakerphone. Her voice on the other end was suddenly quiet as the weight of the news sunk in. Hearing those words as a husband was hard enough – but as a father, watching my daughters learn that their mom's fight was one we might not win was a heartbreak I wasn't prepared for. We walked out of that office in a daze, the world spinning around us while we stood completely paralyzed. I glanced at Cathy, and the devastation was written all over her face. I could see it in her eyes – the heartbreak, the disbelief, the quiet fear of what was to come. After almost 53 years together, I thought we had faced everything life could throw at us. But nothing in our 53 years could have prepared me for that moment.

Dreams Deferred, Paths Unknown

In the days following the diagnosis, everything felt heavier. The boxes we had packed with such excitement now felt like relics from a different life – a life that no longer existed. The custom home we had dreamed of, the spacious kitchen Cathy had been so excited to cook in, the ping-pong room for the grandkids – all of it suddenly felt distant, like echoes of a future we would never fully have.

One of the things we were most excited about was the 40-foot upper deck on our two-story house. From there, we could look out over the Sumner Valley, with a breathtaking view of the Olympic Mountains. We had imagined sitting there together, watching the sun set in the evenings, then seeing the valley light up at night, twinkling below us like a sea of stars. It was so beautiful – everything we had ever wanted. But now, those sunsets felt like they belonged to someone else's story, not ours.

It's strange how quickly life can turn. One moment you're planning family dinners, imagining holidays in a new home, and the next you're sitting in a doctor's office hearing words that shatter every dream you've held close. The plans we had made, the future we had envisioned – they were all slipping away faster than we could hold on.

We had dreamed of growing old in that house – peaceful coffee mornings, laughter echoing through the hallways, grandkids out on the deck. But now, the future we had built felt like a photograph fading at the edges. I didn't know what this new path would hold – I only knew it was nothing like the one we had imagined. The road ahead would be one of uncertainty, surrender, and heartbreak. But somehow, even as our dreams slowly evaporated, God was still holding us.

Study Guide

Bible Study Helps: Reflect and Apply

Chapter One Summary: In this chapter, I shared the moments when my life changed forever – the diagnosis that shattered the dreams Cathy and I had built together. It was a season of excitement and transition: moving into a new home, preparing for a future we had long imagined – only to be met with devastating news that turned everything upside down.

Key Scriptures for Reflection

Proverbs 3:5–6	*"Trust in the LORD with all your heart and lean not on your own understanding; in all your ways acknowledge Him, and He shall direct your paths."*
Romans 8:28	*"And we know that all things work together for good to those who love God, to those who are the called according to His purpose."*
Psalm 34:18	*"The LORD is near to those who have a broken heart and saves such as have a contrite spirit."*

Reflection Questions

1. Have you experienced a time when your future suddenly changed? How did you respond?
2. What emotions surface when you think about the dreams you've lost through grief?
3. How can you hold onto gratitude for the past while also acknowledging the pain of grief?

4. Looking back, can you see any ways God was present in the moments when everything fell apart – even if you didn't recognize it at the time?
5. What do you wish someone had said or done for you when your life took an unexpected turn? How might you offer that to someone else walking through grief?

Going Deeper

Take a few moments to sit with these questions. Don't rush your answers – let them stir your heart and open a conversation between you and God.

- Which Scripture from this chapter speaks to your current season of life? Why?
- What do you think it means that God is with you even when everything feels shattered?

Prayer Prompt

Write a short prayer asking God to meet you in the places where dreams have been lost. Invite Him into your pain, your questions, and your hopes for healing. *(Use the space below to write your prayer:)*

_____

_____

_____

_____

_____

_____

_____

Journal Your Thoughts

Walking Through Anticipatory Grief

Facing the Unknown - The First Days After Diagnosis

GRIEF DOESN'T ALWAYS BEGIN WITH LOSS. Sometimes, it starts long before the final goodbye. This is known as *anticipatory grief* – the mourning that begins the moment you realize someone you love is slipping away. It's a strange kind of grief, one that exists alongside hope, laughter, and even moments of joy. You're holding onto the present while preparing for the inevitable, and that tension can be overwhelming.

For Cathy and me, anticipatory grief began the day we heard the words *Stage IV Ovarian Cancer*. From that moment on, we weren't just living – we were grieving, even as we tried to make the most of the time we had left.

The days after Cathy's diagnosis felt like we were living in a fog. We'd wake up in the morning, and for a brief moment, everything felt normal. But then reality would crash back in, heavy and unavoidable. *Stage IV Ovarian Cancer. No hope.* Those words replayed in my mind like a broken record. But even as they echoed, there was a part of me that clung to the idea of a miracle.

Cathy, ever the strong one, tried to stay positive. "We'll take it one day at a time," she'd say, her voice steady even when her eyes betrayed the fear she felt. I wanted to believe her, to hold onto the possibility that the doctors could be wrong. But deep down, we both knew – we were walking a path we never imagined.

Living in the In-Between - Moments of Normalcy and Fear

There were days when everything felt almost normal. We'd sit on the deck, watching the sunset over the Olympic Mountains, sipping coffee like we always did. For those moments, it was easy to forget about the cancer, to pretend like life was just as it had always been. We laughed, we talked about the grandkids, and for a while, it seemed like we had all the time in the world.

Then there were the other days – the ones when Cathy was too tired to get out of bed, when the weight of what was coming felt like it was suffocating us. Those were the days when I'd find myself staring at her, trying to memorize every detail of Cathy's face, the sound of her voice, knowing that someday soon I wouldn't have those things anymore.

Conversations that Matter - Facing the Hard Topics

As the days went on, Cathy and I found ourselves having conversations we never thought we'd need to have. We talked about everything – the good, the bad, and the heartbreaking. She told me about her hopes for the grandkids, her dreams for our daughters and our son, and the little things she wanted me to remember, like how she taught me to cook some of our favorite meals. She showed me how to make salmon just the way she liked it, how to stir-fry vegetables until they were perfect, and a few other meals we enjoyed together. She wanted me to remember that – so I'd make sure to take care of myself and eat well, even after she was gone.

Our son was part of this journey too, standing beside us, quietly supporting both of us in ways only a son can. He carried his own grief, but never let it overshadow the love and strength he showed for his mom. Seeing him navigate this with us reminded me of how much Cathy and I had poured into our family – and how much they were now pouring back into us.

One night, as we sat in the living room, Cathy reached for my hand. "I'm not afraid of what's next," she whispered. "I just don't want to leave you." Those words broke me in a way I can't explain. I had spent my life protecting her, loving her, walking beside her through every storm. But this was a storm I couldn't shield my wife from.

After nights like that, when Cathy had drifted off to sleep, I'd quietly slip out of bed. I'd walk into the living room, sit down in front of those massive windows overlooking the valley, and just let the tears fall. The view stretched out over the Sumner Valley, peaceful and still, but inside, I was anything but. I sobbed. I prayed. I begged God to heal her, to give us more time. Some nights I'd sit there for what seemed like hours, pouring my heart out in a way I couldn't during the day. Cathy never knew just how many tears I shed in that quiet room, staring out at the lights of the valley, pleading with God to change what felt unchangeable.

Wrestling With God - The Questions That Wouldn't Go Away

In those long, quiet nights, after Cathy had fallen asleep, it wasn't just tears that filled the room – it was questions. *Why her, Lord? Why us? Why now?* I had spent years preaching about faith in the storms, about trusting God's plan even when it didn't make sense. But this? Watching the woman I love slip away a little more each day – it felt like a test I wasn't prepared to take.

At first, there were moments when it seemed like things might turn around. The medical reports showed slight improvements, and I'd cling to any sign of hope, thinking maybe – just maybe – we'd get our miracle. But it wasn't long before the reports started going south. I saw it in Cathy's body even before the doctors confirmed it. She began losing weight rapidly, developing Cachexia – a condition characterized by significant weight loss and muscle wasting, often associated with chronic diseases – her once strong frame becoming frail before my eyes. It was like the life was being drained from her, and no matter how hard I prayed, I couldn't stop it.

Then came the final blow. We were told the cancer had spread – it wasn't just in Cathy's body anymore. She was diagnosed with leptomeningeal disease, meaning the cancer had reached the covering of her brain, her spine, and up and down her back. Hearing those words I felt the ground had been ripped out from under me. I kept asking God, *How much more can she take? How much more can we take?*

I wasn't angry with God – not exactly. But I was confused. I knew He could heal Cathy if He wanted to. I believed in His power, in His goodness. But in the face of her diagnosis, I found myself asking a question I never thought I would: *What if He doesn't? And if He doesn't, what does that mean for the faith I've built my life on?*

The Scriptures That Sustained (and Challenged) Me

In the middle of the hardest nights, when I almost couldn't breathe under the weight of what was happening, I found myself returning to the scriptures I had preached for years. Now they weren't just verses on a page – they were lifelines. One verse that became a constant companion was Psalm 147:3: *"He heals the brokenhearted and binds up their wounds."* I repeated those words over and over again, clinging to the promise that God was close even when I felt so far from Him. Some nights, those words were like a warm blanket, a reminder that we weren't alone in our suffering. Other nights, they were just words – true, maybe, but distant. Still, I kept coming back to them, because even in my doubt, I needed to believe God was near.

The Scriptures That Felt Hollow

But not every Scripture brought comfort. There were times when I'd open my Bible, searching for hope, and instead I felt more lost. Jeremiah 29:11: *"For I know the plans I have for you,' declares the LORD, 'plans to prosper you and not to harm you, plans to give you a hope and a future'"* (NIV). I had shared this verse with countless people over the years, reminding them of God's goodness and faithfulness. But as I watched Cathy's health decline, those words seemed like they belonged to someone else's story – not ours. I wrestled with God in those moments. *How could this be a part of His plan? How could this be for our good?* I knew the promises were true, but they felt distant, like echoes from a place I couldn't quite reach. Faith wasn't easy in those days – it was hard-fought, held onto with every ounce of strength I had left.

The Power of Prayer - Even When It Felt Unanswered

I prayed more during that time than I ever had before – not just the polished prayers I'd spoken from the pulpit, but raw, desperate prayers whispered in the dark. "Lord, heal her! Please, just give us more time!" I begged God for a miracle, for the impossible. And even when the answers didn't come the way I wanted, I kept praying. Not because I always believed He would change the outcome, but because I needed to stay connected to Him, even when I didn't understand His plan.

There were moments when my prayers felt like they were bouncing off the ceiling, unheard and unanswered. But even in those moments, prayer anchored me. It reminded me that God was still there, even if I couldn't feel Him. And sometimes, that was enough to get through another day.

The Shift from Seeking Answers to Seeking Presence

Over time, I realized that I wasn't just looking for answers in Scripture – I was looking for God's presence. I wanted to know He was with us, even if I didn't understand why Cathy had to suffer. Verses like Isaiah 41:10, which I prayed over and over again, became more than promises – they were reminders of God's nearness: *"Fear not, for I am with you; be not dismayed, for I am your God. I will strengthen you and help you; I will uphold you with my righteous right hand."* I stopped expecting God to explain Himself and started trusting He was holding us, even in the silence.

Faith, I realized, wasn't about having all the answers – it was about believing God was still good even when life wasn't.

The Quiet Strength of Cathy's Faith

If there was one thing about Cathy that never changed, it was her faith. From the day of her diagnosis until her final breath, she never once questioned God's love for her. Not even when the pain got worse; not even when the reports kept coming back with bad news. Cathy's faith was rock steady – unshaken, immovable, unwavering. I watched her face suffering with a grace and peace that still amazes me. While I wrestled with questions, she rested in God's goodness. "He's been so good to me," she'd say, even on the hardest days. "He's never left me, and He's not going to start now." I wanted to believe like that. I wanted to hold onto God with the same certainty she did. But there were days when my faith felt fragile compared to hers.

Cathy had a confidence in God's love that was unshakeable. She didn't see herself as someone being abandoned in suffering – she saw herself as someone deeply loved by God. She never asked, "Why me?" She never questioned why this was happening. Instead, she focused on what she knew to be true: That God was faithful, that He was with her, and that His love was constant.

One evening as we sat together in the quiet, she looked at me and said, "I know where I'm going. I know who's waiting for me. And I know that when the time comes, God will give you the strength to keep going." She wasn't afraid. And somehow, her confidence in that moment gave me strength, too.

Cathy's faith wasn't just something she held onto privately – it radiated outward. Our children, our grandchildren, our friends – they all saw it. They saw the way she trusted God without hesitation, the way she spoke about His goodness even when her body was failing. And because she believed so fully, others believed too. Even in the hardest moments, Cathy's peace became an anchor for all of us. She reminded me, time and time again, that suffering didn't change who God was. "He is still good," she'd whisper when I struggled. "He is still faithful," And she meant every word.

Cathy's faith wasn't the kind that shouted – it was quiet, deep, and unwavering. She didn't have to say much for people to know where she stood. She simply lived her faith. Even as her body weakened, her spirit remained strong. And in the end, it wasn't just her faith that carried her – it was her faith that carried me, too.

I had spent my life leading people in faith, but in those final months, Cathy led me. She showed me what it meant to trust without fear, to believe without doubts, and to surrender without hesitation. And even now, I still feel the strength of her faith guiding me.

The Balance Between Hope and Surrender

Every day I prayed for a miracle. I knew God could heal Cathy – there was no doubt in my mind about that. I had seen Him move before, had preached about His power, and watched Him do the impossible. So why not now? Why not us? I refused to stop believing that, even in the Eleventh hour, God could turn this around.

I held on to every bit of good news, every slight improvement in her condition. When she had a little more energy one day, I took it as a sign that maybe – just maybe – things were shifting. I spoke life over her, declaring healing, and prayed without ceasing. I wasn't ready to let go of the hope that she would still be restored.

The Tension - When Hope and Reality Collide

But at the same time, reality was settling in. As much as I wanted to believe in a miracle, I couldn't ignore what was happening in front of me. Cathy was growing weaker. The weight loss, the fatigue – it was undeniable. The reports weren't improving no matter how much I prayed.

I found myself caught between two worlds – one where I believed for healing, and another where I had to prepare for goodbye. I felt like I was walking a tightrope between faith and surrender, between hope and acceptance. And the hardest part? I didn't know which one I was supposed to lean into.

The Moment of Surrender - Letting Go Without Giving Up

At some point – I can't say exactly when – I realized that my prayers started to change. I was still asking for healing, but I was also asking for something else: Peace. Strength. The ability to trust God, no matter what happened next.

I remember sitting with Cathy one evening, holding her hand, watching her drift off to sleep. In that moment, a quiet voice inside me whispered something I had been resisting: *You can trust Me with her.* And for the first time, I truly let go. I still hoped. I still prayed. But I also surrendered. I placed Cathy – her body, her spirit, her future – fully in God's hands. And with that surrender came a strange, unexpected peace.

Accepting That Healing Comes in Different Ways

I had prayed for Cathy's healing, and in my mind, that meant complete restoration – her walking out of this stronger, cancer-free, and ready to enjoy the years we had planned. But I started to realize that healing doesn't always come the way we expect. Sometimes, healing means being freed from pain. Sometimes, healing means stepping into eternity with the One who loves us most. That was hard to accept. But Cathy had already made peace with it long before I did. And in the end, I had to trust that even if healing didn't come on this side of heaven, it was still coming. And that was enough.

Through it all, God spoke something deep into my spirit: "The purpose of God determines when and where He fulfills His promises, whether on earth, or whether in heaven." I had spent so much time asking when the healing would come, but I had to step back and trust *where* God had chosen to fulfill it. Cathy would be healed – completely, fully, eternally. It just wouldn't be in the way I had hoped. But it would still be healing.

Preparing for Goodbye - Embracing Each Day

In those final weeks, time felt different. Every day mattered more; every conversation felt sacred. I knew we were nearing the end, but I wasn't ready. I don't think you're ever ready. Cathy and I had talked about heaven, about eternity. But what do you do when you're still standing here, holding onto someone you love, knowing they're about to leave?

We did our best to embrace each day, even as her body grew weaker. We sat in the quiet together, sometimes talking, sometimes just holding hands, because words weren't always necessary. I watched Cathy soak in the little moments – smiling while talking with the grandkids, closing her eyes as she listened to worship music, holding on to every ounce of life she had left.

The Decision for Comfort Care - A Heartbreaking Transition

About a week before Cathy passed away, our granddaughter Ashley – an oncology nurse at the University of Washington in Seattle – stayed with us for four days, helping care for both of us. She saw the exhaustion in my eyes, the weight I was carrying, and she finally said what I had been afraid to admit: "Papa, you can't keep doing this. You're doing the work of two people, and she needs care beyond what you can provide." Ashley was right. I knew it. But saying it out loud made it real.

A few days later I called my children together – it was Wednesday, June 26th, 2024 – and we made the decision to move Cathy to Comfort

Care at the University of Washington Hospital. It was the hardest decision I had ever made, not because I doubted it was right, but because it meant admitting that our time together at home was over.

The Last Time at Home - A Silent Goodbye

By then, the cancer had taken so much from her. Cathy could no longer walk on her own, and we had to wheel her out in a wheelchair. But before we left our home, my daughter took her out to our back deck one last time. I will never forget that moment – Cathy just sat there, staring out over the beautiful Sumner Valley, with the Olympic Mountains in the distance, looking at the view we had loved so much. She didn't say a word. She just took it all in, knowing she would never return home.

I stood behind her, my heart breaking into pieces. I wanted to freeze time, to keep her here, to hold onto her just a little longer. But I knew – I knew she was already saying goodbye in her own way.

A Sacred Gathering - Surrounded by Love

The day before Cathy passed, something beautiful happened. She was surrounded by 20 family members, all gathered around her bedside, just to let her know how deeply she was loved. It wasn't rushed. It wasn't chaotic. It was sacred. One by one, each person took her hands, and she looked them in the eyes, told them she loved them, and said what was on her heart. There were no words left unsaid. The room was filled with tears, but it was also filled with so much love.

Even in her weakness, Cathy gave everyone a gift that day – the chance to say goodbye, to feel her love one last time, and to carry that with them. It was one of the most powerful moments I've ever witnessed.

The Final Morning - The Tear That Said Everything

The next morning, everything changed. Cathy's pain had become unbearable, and they had to increase the morphine. I never heard her speak again after that, and I didn't know if she could hear me. But I stayed by her side, every single moment. I wasn't going to leave her now. I leaned down, brushed my hand against Cathy's cheek, and whispered, "I love you. You mean everything to me. I don't know if you can hear me, but I want you to know – I never left your side, I stayed with you until the end." I kissed her cheek. And then, a tear fell from her eye onto my lips. In that moment, I knew. She had heard me. She was still with me, even as she was slipping away. About two hours later, I watched her take her last breath.

Study Guide

Bible Study Helps: Reflect and Apply

Chapter Two Summary: Grief doesn't always begin at the moment of loss. It often starts long before. *Anticipatory grief* is the mourning that happens when you realize you're losing someone you love. In this chapter, I reflect on the hard conversations, deep prayers, and the tension between hope and reality as Cathy's condition progressed.

Key Scriptures for Reflection

Psalm 147:3	*"He heals the brokenhearted and binds up their wounds."*
Jeremiah 29:11	*"For I know the plans I have for you," declares the Lord, "plans to prosper you and not to harm you, plans to give you a hope and a future."*
Isaiah 41:10	*"Fear not, for I am with you; be not dismayed, for I am your God. I will strengthen you and help you; I will uphold you with my righteous right hand."*

Reflection Questions

1. What was the hardest part of anticipatory grief for you?
2. How did you balance hope and reality when facing an inevitable loss?
3. Looking back, what would you say to your past self during that time?
4. What role did prayer play in your anticipatory grief? Did your conversations with God change during that time?
5. How did you honor the time you had left with your loved one, even while knowing what was coming?

Going Deeper

Anticipatory grief is filled with tension – between hope and acceptance, between holding on and letting go. Where did you feel this tension most in your own experience?

Prayer Prompt

Write a prayer to God about the emotions you carried during the season of anticipatory grief. Be honest. Tell Him what was hardest. Thank Him for the moments of strength, no matter how small, and ask Him to help you find peace as you continue to heal. *(Use the space below to write your prayer.)*

_____

_____

_____

_____

_____

_____

_____

_____

_____

_____

_____

_____

_____

_____

Journal Your Thoughts

CHAPTER 3

The Power of Scripture in the Darkest Moment

The First Days - A World Without Cathy

THE MORNING AFTER CATHY PASSED, I WOKE TO SILENCE. It was the kind of silence that presses in on you, making the world feel unfamiliar. For over 50 years, I had awakened knowing she was there – whether it was the sound of Cathy moving around in the kitchen, the hum of conversation over morning coffee, or even just the simple warmth of her presence beside me. But that morning? It was just me.

I rolled over in bed, instinctively reaching for her, only to find emptiness. The realization hit me like a wave, knocking the air from my lungs. She's gone. Not at the hospital. Not in the next room. Gone. And for the first time, the house – our home – felt unbearably empty.

I had spent the last several months caring for her, being by her side every moment. And now, my hands felt idle, my purpose unclear. What do you do when the person you've built your life with is no longer there? I sat on the edge of my bed, my hands gripping the mattress, trying to steady myself, but there's no way to steady yourself for a grief like this. One Scripture that kept coming to my mind was when Jesus said, *"I am with you always."* I whispered that verse to myself, trying to convince my heart of what my mind already knew – I wasn't alone, even if I felt like I was.

The Surreal, Disorienting First Days

Grief has a strange way of making time feel both unbearably slow and unnervingly fast. The first few days after Cathy passed were like a fog – moments of deep sorrow mixed with strange clarity. One minute, I was sitting in my chair, lost in thought, and the next I was answering phone calls, making arrangements, responding to messages from friends and family who were grieving alongside me.

People kept asking if I was okay. I didn't know how to answer that. Was I okay? How could I be? My world had changed forever. The person I'd shared my heart, home, laughter, and life with was gone. But I wasn't falling apart either – not in the way people might expect. I was just… existing. Breathing. Moving through each moment – not because I had the strength to, but because life didn't give me a choice.

At first, I struggled to find the words when people asked how I was doing. Sometimes, I'd just nod and say, "I'm hanging in there," or give a half-smile to avoid unraveling in public. But inside, it felt like I was walking through fog – feeling everything and nothing all at once. Then my son Jeff helped put words to what I was truly feeling – words that came from a deeper place than I could articulate at the time. After that, I began to respond with this: "I'm choosing to be happy in honor of Cathy, because I know that is what she would want. And at the same time, I'm continuing to learn how to cope with my grief."

That sentence became more than just a response – it became a life posture. I was learning how to carry both joy and sorrow in the same breath. Choosing happiness didn't mean I wasn't heartbroken. It meant I was trying to live with purpose, even when it hurt. I was trying to laugh again, to be present with the people I loved, to find meaning in small things – not because it was easy, but because Cathy had lived with joy, and I wanted to honor that part of her in how I moved forward.

Grief didn't erase my love for life. It just taught me how sacred every moment really is. And even when the weight of loss pressed heavy on my chest, I knew Cathy would have wanted me to keep going, to keep loving, to keep showing up – for myself, for our family, and for the life we'd both cherished.

Still, the hardest part was the little things. Walking past Cathy's chair and seeing it empty. Realizing I didn't need to cook two meals anymore. Hearing a song she loved and feeling the weight of it settle deep in my chest. Grief isn't just about missing someone in the big moments – it's about feeling their absence in the smallest ones. I remember reading through the Psalms during this time, and one that was especially encouraging was Psalm 30:5: *"Weeping may endure for a night, but joy comes in the morning."* I wanted to believe that joy would return – that this wasn't the end of the story. In those early days, all I could do was hold onto the promise, even when I couldn't yet see the morning.

Clinging to Scripture When Nothing Else Made Sense

I had spent my life reading and preaching Scripture – week after week, sermon after sermon. But after Cathy passed, I found myself holding my Bible in a different way. I wasn't sure if I was reading it as a teacher or as a man desperately needing to hear from God. The words didn't just inform my faith anymore – they were the lifeline holding me together when everything else had come undone. I wasn't reading to prepare a message or lead others. I was reading to survive. Every verse I turned to felt like a breath of air in a room that had suddenly gone dark and quiet. Some days, I could barely read a full chapter. Other days, I would find myself stuck on one verse – repeating it out loud, whispering it like a prayer, hoping it would settle into my spirit and give me the strength to keep going.

There were moments when the pages blurred with tears, when I couldn't make sense of what I was reading. But I kept opening it, kept showing up with my questions and pain, because I knew – even in my confusion – that God's Word was still true, even if I didn't feel it. The scriptures were no longer just theology or memory verses. They became my oxygen. They were the only thing keeping my head above water when the weight of loss threatened to pull me under.

Some verses felt like old friends – comforting and familiar. Others felt distant – words I believed were true but struggled to grasp in my sorrow. I found myself going back to Isaiah 41:10 again and again: *"Fear not, for I am with you; be not dismayed, for I am your God. I will strengthen you and help you, I will uphold you with my righteous right hand."* I whispered those words in the quiet. I spoke them into the empty rooms of our house. And somehow, even in my grief, I knew God was there. I didn't always feel His presence – but I knew it. And sometimes, that knowing was enough.

The Loneliness of Grief - When the House Feels Empty

After the flurry of activity following Cathy's passing subsided, the house settled into a silence that was both foreign and deafening. Every corner, every piece of furniture, seemed to whisper her absence. The kitchen, once filled with the aroma of her cooking and the sound of shared laughter, now felt cold and desolate. Our bedroom, where we had shared countless conversations, dreams, and moments of comfort, now served as a stark reminder of my solitude.

The evenings were the hardest. As the sun dipped below the horizon, a profound sense of loneliness enveloped me. The chair where Cathy sat and read, the spot on the couch where we watched our favorite shows – these places now stood as silent witnesses to a life shared, and a love lost.

The Weight of Unshared Moments

It's often the smallest moments that carry the heaviest weight. Setting the table and realizing there's no need for a second plate. Hearing a song on the radio that she loved and instinctively turning to share a glance, only to remember she's not there. These instances, though seemingly trivial, would pierce through the numbness, bringing the reality of her absence crashing down.

Friends and family were supportive, often checking in and offering their company. Yet, even in their presence, there was an undeniable void. They couldn't fill the space that Cathy had occupied in my life. Their conversation, though comforting, couldn't replace the unspoken understanding and deep connection we had shared.

Seeking Solace in Scripture

In these moments of profound loneliness, I found myself turning to Scripture, not just as a source of comfort, but as my anchor. The Psalms, in particular, resonated deeply with my spirit. David's raw and honest laments mirrored my own feelings of isolation and despair. Psalm 25:16–17 stood out to me: *"Turn to me and be gracious to me, for I am lonely and afflicted. Relieve the troubles of my heart and free me from my anguish."* These verses became a prayer, a plea from the depths of my soul. I would read them aloud, allowing the words to permeate the silence of the house, seeking the comfort and relief they promised.

Psalm 27:10 also provided great solace: *"Though my father and mother forsake me, the Lord will receive me."* That verse reminded me that even in my deepest loneliness, I was not truly alone. God was there – ready to receive me, to offer His unwavering presence when human companionship fell short.

Embracing God's Ever-Present Love

As days turned into weeks, I began to find a strange comfort in the solitude. It was in those quiet, still moments that I felt God's presence most acutely. The loneliness that once felt so overwhelming became the very space where I could meet with Him – pouring out my heart, asking my questions, and finding solace in His unwavering love. I came to understand something sacred: While Cathy's physical presence was no longer with me, God's presence was constant. He was there in the silence, in the emptiness, in the long nights and quiet mornings, offering a peace that truly transcended my understanding.

Psalms 46:1 encapsulated this truth: *"God is our refuge and strength, a very present help in trouble."* I didn't just read those words – I lived them. In my moments of deepest despair, I clung to that promise. God *was* my refuge when I felt unsteady. He *was* my strength when I had none of my own. And in Him, I found the courage to face each lonely day.

When Faith and Grief Collide (The Uncharted Territory of Doubt)

In the aftermath of Cathy's passing, I found myself in unfamiliar territory. As a pastor, I'd spent years counseling others through their grief –

offering words of comfort, praying with them, reassuring them of God's nearness. But now, standing in the epicenter of my own sorrow, those same assurances felt distant, almost hollow.

I questioned God's plan, wondering why a loving Heavenly Father would allow such pain, why healing hadn't come, and why the one I loved most had to suffer. The scriptures that had once wrapped around me like a warm blanket now felt like ink on paper – true, perhaps, but detached from the pain I was walking through.

I felt a profound sense of isolation – not just from those around me, but from the very faith that had once been my anchor. It was as if the foundation I had built my life upon had cracked beneath the weight of my grief. I wasn't walking away from God, but I was certainly wrestling with Him.

The Strength to Pray

Prayer had always been my refuge, a direct line to my Heavenly Father. But in my grief, I found it difficult to pray. Words escaped me, and when they did come, they were often laced with frustration and confusion. I would sit in the quiet of our home, trying to reach out to God, but more often than not, all I could offer were tears. During one of those moments, I remembered the verse from Romans 8:26: *"In the same way, the Spirit helps us in our weakness. We do not know what we ought to pray for, but the Spirit Himself intercedes for us through wordless groans."* That passage became my cornerstone. It reminded me that even when I couldn't form the words, even when all I could do was sit in silence or weep, God still heard me. The Spirit was praying for me when I couldn't pray for myself. That truth gave me comfort, and on some days, it gave me just enough strength to whisper, "God, You know. Help me."

Faith and Grief Co-existing

Through this journey, I began to understand something that changed everything for me: Faith and grief are not mutually exclusive. Experiencing profound sorrow did not mean my faith was weak or broken. In fact, it was in my sorrow that my faith had the opportunity to deepen – to become more honest, more raw, more real. I found comfort in the story of Jesus at Lazarus' tomb. Even though Jesus knew He would raise Lazarus from the dead, He still wept. He didn't rush past the pain. He entered it. He stood in the midst of mourning and allowed His own heart to break. That moment reminded me that mourning is not a failure of faith – it's a holy expression of love and loss. Grief did not separate me from God. In many ways, it drew me closer. Because if Jesus could weep in the face of death, then so could I – and still trust that resurrection, in one form or another, would come.

Embracing the Questions

I learned to embrace my questions and doubts – not as signs of weak faith, but as invitations to be more honest with God. I stopped trying to tie everything up in neat theological bows and instead brought my raw, unfiltered heart before Him. I began to realize that God wasn't intimidated by my pain or confused by my questions. He welcomed them. In doing so, I discovered a more profound sense of His presence. My faith was no longer about having all the answers – it was about trusting in God's goodness, even when life didn't make sense. It was about learning that faith and uncertainty can walk hand in hand, and that God meets us most deeply not in our strength, but in our surrender.

Two scriptures in particular resonated with me during this time: Psalm 34:18: *"The LORD is close to the brokenhearted and saves those who are crushed in spirit.*" I had read that verse for years – but now I was living it. The second was 2 Corinthians 12:9: *"But he said to me, 'My grace is sufficient for you, for my power is made perfect in weakness.'"* Those words took on new meaning. I no longer needed to be strong. I just needed to be surrendered. And God met me there, again and again.

The Scriptures That Became a Lifeline (Finding Refuge in Psalms)

In the quiet moments of my grief, I found myself returning again and again to the Psalms. They became a mirror to my emotions – a sacred space where I didn't have to be strong, where lament and faith could co-exist. The raw honesty of the psalmist resonated deeply, offering words when I had none. One verse that stood out was Psalm 73:26: *"My flesh and my heart may fail, but God is the strength of my heart and my portion forever."* Those words became a balm to my wounded heart. They reminded me that God wasn't asking me to be okay – He was inviting me to rest in His strength when mine was gone. I would read that verse aloud in the stillness of the house, sometimes with tears in my eyes, sometimes just whispering it under my breath. It assured me that God was intimately aware of my pain and actively present in it. He wasn't distant. He was binding up the unseen wounds of my soul, piece by piece, day by day.

Embracing the Promise of Comfort

Jesus' words in the Beatitudes took on a whole new meaning during this time. I had read them countless times, taught them in sermons, quoted them at funerals. But now, I wasn't standing at a pulpit – I was sitting in the ashes of loss. And His promise in Matthew 5:4 – *"Blessed are those who mourn, for they will be comforted"* – landed differently. It wasn't just a beautiful phrase from the Sermon on the Mount. It was a fortress of hope.

For the first time, I wasn't reading it for someone else – I was reading it for *me*. And in that moment, I realized something sacred: Jesus sees mourners. He doesn't overlook them. He blesses them. He draws near. I began to find solace in that truth – that my mourning was not invisible or meaningless. It was seen. It mattered. His words gave me permission to grieve without guilt, to hurt without shame, and to trust that comfort was coming – even if I couldn't yet see it. It didn't erase the pain, but it reminded me that God enters into it. Jesus doesn't just comfort from a distance; He walks into the sorrow with us, sits with us in our pain, and whispers hope into our broken places. This verse became a rock-solid foundation in my soul – a reassurance that my sorrow was not in vain, and that divine comfort was not just possible, it was promised.

Casting Anxieties Upon Him

In moments when anxiety threatened to overwhelm me – when the weight of the unknown, the ache of absence, and the fear of the future closed in – I found solace in Peter's gentle exhortation: *"Cast all your anxieties on Him, because He cares for you"* (1 Peter 5:7). I had read that verse for years, even shared it with others in difficult seasons. But now, the word *cast* suddenly meant more to me than ever before. It wasn't a casual setting down of worries.

It was a deliberate, even desperate act – laying the full weight of my fear, pain, and grief into the hands of a God who could actually carry it.

Some days, casting my anxiety on the Lord looked like whispered prayers through tears. Other days, it was silent moments sitting in my chair, heart racing, saying, *God, I don't know how to do this.* And still other days, it was scribbling down the things I couldn't say out loud and placing them, in faith, before Him.

This verse reminded me that I wasn't alone in my struggles – that I wasn't expected to carry the burden of grief by myself. God wasn't distant. He was attentive. Present. Caring. The kind of caring that sees the empty hands, hears the quiet sobs in the dark, and leans in with compassion. Even now, I don't always feel anxiety leave instantly when I pray. But I know this: Every time I cast my cares on Him, He meets me there. Not with all the answers, but with His peace. And sometimes, that's exactly what I need most.

The Assurances of God's Presence

The promise of God's unwavering presence became a cornerstone of my faith during this season. I clung to the assurance that even in the valley of the shadow of death, I was not walking alone. Grief can feel like a long, lonely road – silent, heavy, filled with shadows of what used to be. But in that darkness, God's presence became my light, sometimes dim and flickering, but always there.

Psalm 23:4 says it so clearly: *"Even though I walk through the valley of the shadow of death, I will fear no evil, for You are with me; Your rod and Your staff, they comfort me."* I had recited that verse at countless funerals over the years. But now, I wasn't reading it for someone else – I was walking it. And the words didn't fall flat. They reached into the depths of my sorrow and gently reminded me that God doesn't just meet us on mountaintops – He walks with us through the valleys.

There were days when the valley felt never-ending – when I couldn't see a way forward and fear threatened to take hold. But I kept returning to that promise: *"You are with me."* Not *You were,* or *You might be* – but *You are.* Present. Active. Faithful. His rod and staff weren't just symbols of protection and guidance – they became real to me. Sometimes, I felt them like a steady hand on my back. Other times, I trusted in them without feeling a thing, choosing to believe that He was guiding me even in the silence.

This verse served as a constant reminder that God's presence is not limited by circumstances. He's not absent in grief. He's not waiting on the other side of sorrow. He's *in* it – with us, beside us, sustaining us one breath at a time.

The Hope of Eternal Reunion

Paul's words to the Corinthians began to echo in my heart in a new way during this season. They weren't just theology anymore – they were personal. They carried a forward-looking hope that helped lift my eyes beyond the ache of the present moment. 2 Corinthians 4:17 says, *"For our light and momentary troubles are achieving for us an eternal glory that far outweighs them all."* At first, that verse felt impossible to grasp. Light and momentary? My pain felt anything but that. It felt heavy. Endless. But the more I sat with Paul's words, the more I realized what he was pointing toward. He wasn't minimizing suffering – he was magnifying eternity.

This verse helped me reframe what I was going through. It didn't erase the sorrow, but it reminded me that this life is not the whole story. There's something coming – a reunion, a restoration, a glory – that will make the weight I'm carrying now seem light by comparison. And that's not because grief is small – it's because eternity is vast. Because heaven is real. Because one day, all that has been lost will be made whole again in Christ.

That perspective helped me breathe again. It gave me permission to grieve deeply, while also hoping boldly. It reminded me that Cathy's life didn't end – it simply changed location. And someday, when God writes the final chapter, there will be no more goodbyes. No more pain. Just joy. Just presence. Just eternal glory that far outweighs them all.

The Turning Point - When Scriptures Moved from Words to Healing

In the weeks following Cathy's passing, there was an evening I'll never forget – a night when the weight of my sorrow became almost unbearable. The house was silent, but the silence didn't feel peaceful. It felt hollow. Every creak of the floor, every empty chair, every room we once filled with laughter echoed with absence. The stillness was deafening. I sat there in the dim light, swallowed by grief, and for the first time, I felt like I was beginning to sink. Not just emotionally, but spiritually. It was a depth of despair I hadn't yet experienced.

Out of sheer desperation – not out of discipline or routine – I reached for my Bible. My hands were unsteady as I opened it, not even knowing where to turn. I wasn't searching for a sermon or a familiar passage – I was just looking for something to hold onto. Anything. I landed in the Gospel of Matthew, and my eyes were drawn like a magnet to the words of Jesus: *"Come to Me, all you who are weary and burdened, and I will give you rest. Take my yoke upon you and learn from Me, for I am gentle and humble in heart, and you will find rest for your souls. For My yoke is easy and My burden is light"* (Matthew 11:28–30, NIV).

I read those words slowly. Then again. And again. They didn't feel like verses on a page. They felt like an invitation – personal, direct, alive. It was as if Jesus Himself was sitting in the room with me, speaking those words into the very places I had tried to keep hidden. My soul was weary. My heart was burdened. And somehow, even in the middle of my grief, I felt seen.

As I meditated on that passage, something unexpected happened. A profound sense of peace washed over me – not all at once, but like gentle waves on a restless shore. The burdens that had been so suffocating began to shift. Not disappear – but lighten. It felt as though Jesus was lifting them with me, not leaving me to carry them alone.

For the first time since Cathy's departure, I sensed a glimmer of hope. A flicker of rest. A promise that even in the darkest valley, I was not abandoned. That night didn't erase my pain – but it marked the beginning of healing. The Word of God became more than words – it became presence, promise, and peace. And that moment became a turning point in my grief, reminding me that even in sorrow, I could still encounter the Savior.

A Shift from Despair to Hope

This encounter marked a turning point in my grieving process. Something shifted that night. It wasn't dramatic or loud, but it was deep and unmistakable. The words I had read in desperation became a doorway into something far more sacred – a living conversation with God. Scripture was no longer a collection of verses I had memorized or preached. It became a voice. A companion. A well of comfort that met me in the depths of my sorrow.

The Bible, a book of truths I had once taught to others, became a lifeline for my own soul. These sacred words didn't just offer me comfort – they carved out a pathway to healing. They reminded me that lament is holy, that sorrow is allowed, and that God's love and compassion reach deeper than any pain I could feel. While the ache of losing Cathy never

42

truly left, it became wrapped in something stronger: The unshakeable presence of God who weeps with us and walks beside us.

Room to Breathe Again

There was a moment during those dark days when the sorrow threatened to snatch away my breath. The ache of Cathy's absence pressed on me from every side. I wasn't just emotionally overwhelmed – I felt physically crushed by the weight of it all. In desperation, I turned to Scripture, not knowing exactly what I needed, only that I needed something beyond myself to survive the day. That's when I came across Psalm 21:1. *"The king shall have joy in Your strength, O LORD; and in Your salvation how greatly shall he rejoice."* At first, it felt almost unreachable – joy seemed like a foreign concept in the middle of so much pain. But then the Lord opened my eyes to something I had never seen before.

I discovered that one of the Hebrew meanings of the word *salvation* is *room to breathe*. In that instant, it felt like God had stepped into the room and lifted the weight off my chest. I literally felt myself exhale, as if I had been holding my breath without realizing it. And then came His gentle whisper: *"I'm not going to let this crush you. I will carry you through."*

I will never forget that moment. It wasn't just a verse – I experienced it. The Word of God became breath to me. That verse became more than truth – it became presence, assurance, and space. God wasn't asking me to be strong. He was inviting me to breathe. I didn't have to force joy or rush through my sorrow. I simply had to trust that His strength would hold me, His salvation would give me space, and His love would see me through. In that sacred moment, I knew I was not alone, and I would not be undone.

Embracing the Journey Ahead

From that moment on, I approached Scripture with a renewed heart. It wasn't about studying anymore – it was about relationship. Each passage became an invitation to connect with my Heavenly Father in the rawness of my grief. I no longer opened my Bile to prepare a message for others. I opened it to hear something for myself – to find solace when I was empty, guidance when I felt lost, and strength when I didn't think I could face another day without Cathy.

The Bible transformed into a wellspring of healing. It didn't erase the loneliness, but it reminded me that I was never truly alone. God's Word became my companion at the table where one chair now sat empty. It walked with me through quiet mornings and long nights. It gave me permission to feel everything I was feeling – and yet, it always pulled me back to the promises of God's goodness, even in the midst of sorrow.

There was no lightning bolt, no instant fix. Just a steady, quiet rebuilding of faith through the gentle, faithful whispers of Scripture. Over time, I realized that while I had lost my beloved partner, I hadn't lost my purpose. And I hadn't lost the God who had walked with us both for so many years. Even in the depths of grief, He was still writing my story. Though one season was ending, a quiet hope was beginning to take shape. And in the sacred space between sorrow and healing, I learned that God doesn't just speak in our strength – He often speaks most clearly in our silence and surrender.

Study Guide

Bible Study Helps: Reflect and Apply

Chapter Three Summary: Grief can shake the very foundation of faith. In this chapter, I share the scriptures that sustained me in the darkest moments – when I was overwhelmed by sorrow, wrestling with doubt, fear, and the silence of unanswered prayers. I had to decide whether I would cling to the promises of God or let grief define my faith. This chapter is about that decision – and how, even when my faith wavered, God's Word remained steady. It's about how Scripture became not just a source of comfort, but a lifeline.

Key Scriptures for Reflection

Matthew 11:28–30	*"Come to Me, all you who are weary and burdened, and I will give you rest…" (NIV).*
2 Corinthians 4:17	*"For our light and momentary troubles are achieving for us an eternal glory that far outweighs them all" (NIV).*
Psalm 23:4	*"Yea, though I walk through the valley of the shadow of death, I will fear no evil; for You are with me…"*

Reflection Questions

1. Have you struggled with faith during grief? What emotions did you experience?
2. Which Scripture or spiritual truths have helped you the most in this season?
3. How has your perspective on God changed through grief?
4. When was the last time Scripture felt personal, like God was speaking directly to you? What was that moment like?

5. If you're in a season of silence or struggle, what would it look like to approach God with honesty instead of performance?

Going Deeper

Grief doesn't just affect our emotions – it challenges the very framework of our faith. In this chapter, we saw that God invites us to bring our sorrow, doubt, and questions into His presence, not hide them. Scripture is more than information – it becomes transformation when we allow it to meet us where we truly are. As you reflect, consider what it looks like to move from reading the Bible as routine to receiving it as relationship. What might change if you stopped striving to "feel better" and instead allowed God's Word to simply sit with you, speak to you, and strengthen you – even in the silence?

Prayer Prompt

Write a prayer from where you are right now – whether it's full of questions, hope, sorrow, or a mix of all three. Ask God to meet you in the tension between grief and faith. Use this space to be completely honest with Him. You don't need perfect words – just real ones. *(Use the space below to write your prayer.)*

Journal Your Thoughts

CHAPTER 4

The Healing Power of Family – Walking Through Grief Together

The First Weeks Without Cathy - A Family That Wouldn't Let Go

GRIEF IS DISORIENTING. It turns familiar spaces into hollow reminders of what's no longer there. The first time I walked into our home alone after Cathy passed, I was overwhelmed by the silence. No sound of her voice calling from the other room. No movement in the kitchen where she always made sure I was well-fed and cared for. No subtle music playing in the background. Just stillness. Heavy, unrelenting stillness.

I struggled being in the house alone. Everything felt too big, too empty – too full of memories that screamed of my loss. Every corner held traces of her laughter, her love, her quiet presence. And without her, it felt like the very heartbeat of our home had stopped. But my family knew this. Somehow, they sensed the weight I was carrying – and in those first days and weeks, they refused to let me carry it alone.

For six weeks straight, my children and grandchildren made sure I was never by myself. Not once. They didn't just offer words of comfort

– they rearranged their lives to be present. My daughters, Heidi and Jamie, had me over for dinner constantly. They made sure I was eating. They made sure I was talking. They filled their homes with warmth and welcome, even when their own hearts were grieving. I was at their houses often enough that it began to feel like a shared rhythm of healing – we were walking through the loss together.

My son Jeff checked in daily. Sometimes with a phone call, other times with a text just to say, "How are you doing today, Dad?" But often, our conversations lasted an hour or more – conversations filled with memories, wisdom, tears, and reminders that grief was a journey, not a sentence. He didn't try to fix my pain. He simply walked through it with me. To this day, those calls continue. They are not just check-ins – they are anchors.

And then there were my grandchildren. Teenagers and young adults – each navigating their own lives, but still taking the time to reach out. I would get text messages throughout the day: "I love you, Papa." "Thinking about you." "Just wanted you to know you're not alone." Sometimes they stopped by unannounced, sat beside me, and said almost nothing. But their presence was everything. It told me that love doesn't end with death. It told me that Cathy's legacy – our legacy – was alive in them.

I can say without hesitation or exaggeration: I would not have survived those first weeks without my family. Their love wrapped around me like a safety net when I was falling apart. My three children – grieving their own mother – put their pain on hold at times to lift me up. They became my shelter, my strength, and in many ways, my healing began in their arms.

Looking back, I realize those early acts of love – those dinners, calls, hugs, texts, and quiet visits – formed the foundation for my recovery. They reminded me that I wasn't walking through this valley alone. That

I still had people who needed me. Who loved me. Who were willing to walk through the darkest season of life together, one day at a time.

Moments That Meant Everything

Grief isn't just felt in the big, public moments – it shows up in the quiet, unexpected ones. And healing, I've come to realize, often begins there too. It's not always in the grand gestures that we feel the most comfort, but in the small, sacred moments that sneak up on us and speak directly to our hearts.

One afternoon, while I was visiting my daughter Jamie's house, my grandson JJ came over to me. He didn't say much. He just walked up, wrapped his arms around me, and said, "Papa, I just want you to know that I love you and I'm always here for you." That simple act, that one sentence, reached a place in me that was still raw and hurting. He didn't try to fix anything. He just loved me. And in that moment, it was enough. It meant everything.

Another time, while sitting with some of my grandchildren, one of them looked at me and asked, "Papa, do you think Grammy's watching us from heaven?" I paused, knowing exactly how Cathy would've answered that question – with warmth, joy, and unwavering faith. I smiled and said, "I do. And I think she's smiling at you right now." Their faces lit up with a quiet comfort, and I knew in that moment that Cathy's influence – her love – was still living and active in their hearts. Those questions, those moments of wonder, weren't just comfort – they were bridges between generations, faith, and memory.

There were also the moments of practical love that meant more than words could say. One day, Heidi and Jamie spent hours with me going through every detail of Cathy's burial service at Tahoma National

Cemetery and her Celebration of Life Service at New Life Church in Covington, Washington. It wasn't easy work – sorting through photos, creating a tribute video, choosing music, and reviewing every part of the service to make sure it honored Cathy's life in the most beautiful way. We laughed, cried, paused, and remembered together. Those hours weren't just preparation – they were part of the grieving and part of the healing.

My son Jeff poured wisdom into my life during that time. Jeff's insights – steady, clear, thoughtful – helped me navigate decisions I didn't want to make. His voice became one of the strongest pillars in my grief. I don't think he fully realizes how incredibly wise he is, or how his calm presence brought peace to my heart when everything else felt uncertain.

And through it all, both of my daughters carried their own sorrow while somehow never letting go of me. They were grieving their mom, yet they showed up again and again – offering strength when I had none, helping me sort through details when I couldn't focus, giving hugs that spoke more than words ever could.

Looking back, I am overwhelmed by the love my children and grandchildren have shown me. Their presence. Their actions. Their quiet determination to hold me up from the moment Cathy left this earth. They didn't wait for me to ask for help – they stepped in and stayed close. In doing so, they didn't just support me… they became part of my healing.

Grieving Together and Individually

One of the most important things I've learned on this journey is that grief is deeply personal – no two people grieve the same way, even when they're grieving the same loss. While we walked through this season as a family, each of us carried our grief differently. Some of us needed to talk about Cathy often – sharing memories, telling stories, keeping her name woven into every conversation. There was healing in speaking her name aloud, in letting the sound of it still fill the room.

Others grieved in quiet reflection, needing space to sit in their sorrow privately. Their love didn't express itself through words but through silence, through tears behind closed doors, through quiet acts of remembrance. And that was okay too. Grief doesn't follow a script. It doesn't move in straight lines. It comes in waves, and each wave looks a little different for each person who's riding it.

As a family, we gave one another permission to grieve in our own ways. We didn't expect anyone to feel the same things at the same time. But what mattered most is that we never let each other grieve alone. We showed up. We stayed connected. We made space for both conversation and silence, for laughter and tears, for being together and being apart. That kind of shared grace made all the difference.

There were moments, especially around the holidays – Thanksgiving, Christmas – when Cathy's absence felt even more overpowering. The traditions she started, the meals she cooked, the way she made every gathering feel warm and full of love… all of it was missed. But instead of avoiding the pain, we leaned into it. We chose to speak her name, to talk about her, to keep her memory alive. I remember one moment in particular – sitting with my children and grandchildren and saying, "You know, your mom and your Grammy would be so proud of us right now. We're together. We're grieving well. And we're remembering her in the way she deserves to be remembered." There were tears, but there was peace too.

Grief is not something you "get over." It's something you learn to walk through. And while the pace and the path may look different for each of us, the beauty of our family is that we've chosen to walk through it side by side. Some days we carry one another. Other days we simply walk quietly next to each other. But we keep walking. Together.

The Role of Family in Encouraging Faith

Losing Cathy didn't destroy my faith – but it did make me wrestle with God in ways I never had before. My belief in His goodness remained intact, but I found myself weighed down with questions I couldn't answer. Not theological questions, but deeply personal ones. Why now? Why her? Why would God allow her to suffer after we had faithfully followed Him for so many years? Why would He bless us with the chance to build our dream home – a place Cathy was so excited about – only to take her before she could truly enjoy it?

These weren't accusations. They were cries from a heart that was grieving, trying to reconcile the pain of loss with the promises I had clung to for decades. I didn't doubt that God was good – I just didn't understand how His goodness fit into *this*. There were nights when I sat in silence, staring at the ceiling, whispering, "Lord, I trust You...but I don't get this." And He met me there – in the questions, in the tension.

But I wasn't wrestling alone. My family became the voice of faith when mine was weary. In ways they probably didn't realize, they spoke truth to me when I needed to hear it most. My children – each grieving the loss of their mother – still found the strength to remind me of God's faithfulness. They didn't offer clichés or pat answers. They offered presence. They offered scripture. They reminded me of what Cathy believed and lived for. They pointed me back to the truth, again and again.

And my grandchildren... they became tangible expressions of God's love. A hug at just the right time. A text message saying, "*I love you, Papa.*" A question about heaven that reminded me this life isn't all there is. They may not have known it, but God was using them to minister to me, to pull me gently toward hope when grief clouded my vision.

It's one thing to say, "God will never leave you." It's another thing entirely to feel that truth through the steady, unshakable love of family. That's what I experienced. My faith didn't weaken in this season. If anything, it grew stronger – not because I had all the answers, but because I was held by people who kept pointing me to the One who does.

Looking back, I know without a doubt that part of the strength I stand on today didn't come from within me – it came from the love of a family who refused to let me forget the truth. They grieved with me, wrestled with me, sat in silence with me, and gently reminded me, even in the darkest moments, that God was still good and He was still with us.

A Family's Love as a Reflection of God's Love

If there's one thing I've learned in this season, it's this: God often reveals His love through the people He places in our lives. When my heart was too heavy to lift, when days blurred together and the nights were long and silent, it was the people who showed up that reminded me God hadn't left.

I have no doubt that my children and grandchildren were God's way of holding me up when I didn't have the strength to stand. Their love didn't fix my grief – but it gave me something sacred to lean on. In them, I saw God's compassion. In their hugs, I felt His nearness. In their faithfulness, I witnessed His heart. God didn't rush me through my sorrow. He didn't push me to move on or pretend I was okay. He simply showed up – through them – and that made all the difference.

Maybe you're grieving right now. Maybe you've lost someone so dear that you can't imagine how to move forward. Maybe the silence is louder than it's ever been. If that's where you are, let me encourage you: You don't have to walk this road alone. Lean on the people around you. If you have family, let them in. Let them love you. Let them grieve with you. If you don't have family close by, open your heart to the people God has placed in your life – friends, neighbors, your church family. There are more people who care than you think. And even more important, there is a God who sees you and surrounds you with love in ways you might not expect.

Cathy may no longer be physically with us, but her love is still here – alive and well in our children and grandchildren, in the way they care for one another, in the way they remember her, in the way they continue to walk forward with faith and grace. That, to me, is one of the greatest reflections of God's love I've ever experienced. It's not loud. It's not flashy. It's steady, faithful, and full of grace.

And that's what love is. That's what God is like. Present in the quiet. Strong in the ordinary. Holding us through the hardest moments, not with answers, but with presence. And through the love of my family, I've come to know His presence more deeply than ever before.

Study Guide

Bible Study Helps: Reflect and Apply

Chapter Four Summary: Grief is personal, and it also affects everyone around us. In this chapter, I reflect on the role of family in my healing journey – the ways they supported me, how we grieved differently, and how we learned to lean on each other even when grief felt isolating. Through their presence, love, and faith, my family reminded me that I wasn't alone – and that God often shows his love through the people He places in our lives.

Key Scriptures for Reflection

Romans 12:15	*"Rejoice with those who rejoice, and weep with those who weep."*
Ecclesiastes 4:9–10	*"Two are better than one … For if they fall, one will lift up his companion."*
John 13:34	*"A new commandment I give to you, that you love one another; as I have loved you, that you also love one another."*
2 Corinthians 1:3–4	*"The God of all comfort, who comforts us in all our tribulation, that we may be able to comfort those who are in any trouble…"*
Psalm 68:6	*"God sets the solitary in families; He brings out those who are bound into prosperity."*

Reflection Questions

1. How has your family – or someone close to you – played a role in your healing journey?
2. In what ways do you see people around you grieving differently? How can you honor those differences with compassion?

3. When have you experienced the love of God through someone else's presence, support, or words?
4. If you've felt alone in your grief, what steps might you take to lean on someone – or let someone in?
5. What legacy of love, faith, or strength has your family passed on to you that gives you comfort today?

Going Deeper

Grief may feel isolating, but God often surrounds us with people who reflect His love in tangible ways. Whether through a shared memory, a hug, a listening ear, or a quiet presence, these moments become reminders that we're not walking this road alone. Family doesn't always mean blood – it means community, connection, and care. Ask yourself: Who has God placed in my life to walk with me? And how can I also be a reflection of His love to someone else who may be hurting?

Prayer Prompt

Write a prayer thanking God for the people who have walked with you in your grief. Be honest about where you still feel lonely or overwhelmed. Ask Him to help you continue receiving love from others – and to help you offer it freely, even in your own sorrow. *(Use the space below to write your prayer.)*

_____

_____

_____

_____

_____

_____

Journal Your Thoughts

CHAPTER 5

Getting to the Other Side of Grief - When Wisdom Becomes a Lifeline

A Life-Changing Realization: I Didn't Understand Grief

BEFORE CATHY'S PASSING, I THOUGHT I UNDERSTOOD GRIEF. I really did. As a pastor, I had walked with countless families through seasons of loss. I sat with them in hospital rooms and living rooms. I prayed over them at gravesides and offered words of comfort from the pulpit during funeral services. I spoke about heaven, hope, and healing with a sincere heart, believing every word I said. But when the grief became mine – when I was no longer the one offering support, but the one shattered by loss – I realized how little I truly understood. No book, no sermon, no amount of ministry experience could have prepared me for what it actually felt like to lose the person I loved most in this world.

Grief wasn't just sadness – it was a complete disorientation. I felt like I had lost my bearings. Everything familiar felt foreign. The routines we shared, the conversations, the small daily rituals – all of it vanished in an instant, and I was left walking through rooms that once held laughter but now echoed with silence. The ache wasn't just emotional; it was physical. It settled deep in my chest, in my stomach, in my bones. I was exhausted – not just from crying, but from carrying the weight of a sorrow I couldn't put into words.

I quickly came to a humbling conclusion: I didn't know how to grieve. Not really. I had helped others through it, but now I was the one who needed help. And that's when God used my son Jeff to do something that changed everything. Sensing how lost I felt, he took the initiative and sent me four books on grief. At the time, I don't think even he realized how much those books would mean to me – how they would become lifelines in the most difficult season of my life.

Each one arrived like a quiet friend – offering words when I had none, insights I didn't know I needed, and wisdom that slowly, gently helped me begin to breathe again. In the next section, I'll share what those books were and why they had such a powerful impact on my healing. But first, I'll say this: Sometimes, the most life-changing moments come not from answers, but from the wisdom and compassion of others who have walked the road before you.

The Gift That Changed Everything: Four Books on Grief

My son saw the depth of my pain. He didn't try to talk me out of it or offer empty words of comfort. Instead, he did something far more powerful – he responded with insight and compassion. He instinctively knew I needed more than just support – I needed guidance. Something to help me find my footing when everything beneath me felt like it had collapsed. He sent me four books, not as a solution, but as a balm of healing.

At first, I didn't realize just how much they would come to mean to me. But slowly, page by page, those books became companions in my sorrow. They didn't erase the pain – but they gave me language for it. They helped me process what felt senseless. They gave me permission to grieve deeply without feeling like I was doing it wrong. And most of all, they reminded me that hope and sorrow can coexist. Each of these books met me in a different place – one spoke to my theology, another to my emotions, another to my faith, and another to my very identity as a grieving husband and believer. I would sit in my chair, reading slowly, often stopping to underline a sentence or close the book just to let the words sink in. These were not just resources. They were sacred tools of healing, sent at just the right time.

And I thank God for Jeff. His quiet act of care was more than just thoughtful – it was prophetic. He saw what I couldn't articulate and gave me something that changed the course of my healing. In the pages of those books, I began to see that I wasn't alone. Others had walked this path. Others had struggled, doubted, and found light again. If they could, maybe I could too.

The Impact of Each Book

A Grief Observed - C.S. Lewis

The first book I opened was *A Grief Observed* by C.S. Lewis – and right away, it met me in my brokenness. Lewis's words didn't offer easy answers or polished theology. What they offered was honest, unfiltered humanity. It was like reading someone else's journal while realizing it could have been your own. His raw honesty gave me the courage to face my own doubts. He didn't hold back from expressing confusion, anger, or even spiritual despair. For a man so revered in Christian thought, his transparency made me feel less alone in my own struggle with God during those early days of grief. I wasn't losing faith – but I was wrestling with it. And Lewis gave me permission to do just that.

63

One line in particular struck me like a lightning bolt: "No one ever told me that grief felt so like fear." That sentence brought tears to my eyes, because I hadn't known how to describe what I was feeling until I read it. It wasn't just sadness – it was anxiety, disorientation, vulnerability. It felt like the floor had dropped out from under me. And Lewis put words to those emotions in a way that no one else had. Through his reflections, I learned that grief isn't neat and tidy. It's messy, unpredictable, and deeply personal. It doesn't follow a timeline or respect our expectations. And that realization was freeing. I didn't have to pretend to be okay. I didn't have to rush the process. I could let grief take its course – because even in its chaos, God was still present.

Lewis didn't tie everything up with a bow by the end of the book. And that, too, was comforting. Because real grief doesn't end in resolution – it ends in surrender. *A Grief Observed* didn't give me all the answers, but it helped me find language for the ache, and in doing so, it became the first step in learning how to grieve.

Comfort For the Grieving Spouse's Heart - Gary Roe

This book reminded me of something I hadn't fully understood until I was in the middle of it – grieving as a spouse is different. It's not just the pain of losing someone you love. It's the loss of your closest companion, your daily rhythm, your safe place. It's losing the person who knew your quirks, shared your inside jokes, understood your moods without explanation. I wasn't just mourning Cathy – I was mourning the life we had built, the future we had dreamed about, the small sacred routines that made up our days.

The grief of a spouse isn't always loud. Sometimes, it's found in the sight of an empty chair, the sound of only one plate hitting the dinner table, the realization that no one will be there waiting for you when you come home. It's the aching absence of someone who once filled every space with their presence – even when they weren't saying a word. It's the presence of absence, and it's suffocating at times.

Gary Roe's book understood that in a way few others did. His words weren't clinical or detached – they were personal, tender, and filled with compassion. It felt as though he wasn't writing about grief; he was writing *from* it.

His honesty about the weight of losing a spouse helped me feel seen and understood. He acknowledged the disorientation, the loneliness, the invisible wounds that others often can't see but we feel every single day.

There was something sacred about the way Roe addressed the emotional and spiritual battle that comes with spousal grief. He reminded me that it's okay *not* to be okay. That grief isn't something to fix or move on from – but something to live with, carry, and bring before God honestly. And he gave me the language to do that. His prayers, scattered throughout the pages, became prayers I whispered as my own. Simple, raw, and real. *"God, I miss her. I don't know how to live this life without her. But I know You're here. Help me breathe again."* That kind of prayer doesn't tie up sorrow with a bow – it invites God into it. And that made all the difference.

Gary's words became like a steady friend walking beside me through the long nights and quiet days. He helped me realize that the deep emptiness I felt wasn't something to be ashamed of – it was evidence of deep love. And because of that love, I didn't have to rush through grief. I could honor it. I could honor Cathy. And in doing so, I could slowly begin to heal.

Getting to the Other Side of Grief - Susan Zonnebelt-Smeenge and Robert C. DeVries

Out of all the books I received, this one was the one I kept returning to – again and again. Then I picked it up a second time. But it was during the third time through that something began to shift inside me. I don't know what changed – maybe my heart had softened just enough, or maybe the fog of grief had lifted slightly – but suddenly, the words on those pages began to land in a way they hadn't before. This book became more than just a resource. It became a road map through terrain I didn't know how to navigate. It didn't minimize my pain, but it helped me see that grief wasn't a permanent place of paralysis. It introduced me to the idea that healing isn't about "moving on" or forgetting. Healing, they explained, is about learning how to carry both love and loss – together. Not either/or. Both/and. That was a revelation for me.

Until that point, I think a part of me felt like moving forward might dishonor Cathy's memory. Like healing somehow meant letting go of what we had built together. But this book gently, wisely reminded me that honoring her life didn't mean staying stuck in sorrow. It meant finding a new way to live while carrying her love forward. That realization didn't take the pain away – but it gave it a new purpose.

The authors didn't offer platitudes. They offered practical wisdom, born from experience, grounded in faith. They helped me understand the different stages and layers of grief – not as a linear process, but as a series of waves, cycles, and moments that needed attention, grace, and time. They showed me that what I was feeling was normal, even when it felt anything but.

Most of all, the authors painted a picture of what life on the other side of deep grief could look like. Not perfect. Not pain-free. But purposeful. Hopeful. Redeemed. That vision stirred something in me I hadn't felt in a while – the desire to live again. To find meaning. To pursue healing, not just for my own sake, but so that I could continue to show up for my family, for others who were hurting, and for the calling God still had on my life.

I underlined entire paragraphs. I wrote notes in the margins. I remember setting the book down more than once with tears in my eyes, thinking, *This… this is what I've needed to hear.* It was like someone had taken my hand and said, "You're not crazy. You're not alone. And you're going to make it through this."

To this day, I recommend this book to others who are grieving. Not because it offers all the answers – but because it helps you ask the right questions, and it walks with you gently toward hope. It truly helped me begin to see that getting to the other side of grief doesn't mean leaving your love behind – it means carrying it forward with purpose, faith, and strength.

Through a Season of Grief - Bill Dunn and Kathy Leonard

This book – *Through a Season of Grief* – turned out to be one of the most valuable resources I received. It was also one of the recommended readings from the GriefShare group I attended, and together the book and the group became an emotional life preserver during the time when everything in my life felt adrift.

What made this book so meaningful was its devotional format. It wasn't long chapters or heavy theology – it was simple, daily reflections. Just enough to meet me where I was without overwhelming me. Some days, I would read the day's entry and nod quietly, comforted by the truth it offered. Other days, the words felt like they were written just for me, echoing my pain, validating my emotions, and gently pointing me toward hope.

Grief is exhausting – emotionally, mentally, even physically. And in that exhaustion, it's easy to forget to care for your own soul. This book became a way for me to do just that. Each page helped me slow down, breathe, and reflect. It gave me permission to feel what I was feeling and encouragement to take one small step forward, even if that step was simply *getting through the day*. And on the days when I didn't even want to open a book, its gentle tone never condemned me – it waited patiently until I was ready.

GriefShare itself was an incredible gift. Walking into that room, sitting with others who were also navigating the pain of loss, made me feel less alone. But this book allowed those truths to follow me home. It reinforced what I was learning each week. It helped carry the wisdom from our group sessions into the quiet spaces of my own life – into the early mornings, the lonely evenings, the moments when I felt the ache of Cathy's absence more deeply than I could describe.

One of the most healing realizations this book brought me was that grief comes in seasons. That phrase reminded me that just as winter eventually gives way to spring, the sharpest edges of sorrow would, in time, soften. Healing wouldn't come all at once – but it would come. Not through rushing, not through pretending, but through *staying with the process*. Through bringing my pain before God and allowing Him to walk with me through it.

I still remember specific devotions that helped me get through particularly hard days – words that spoke to my fatigue, my doubt, even my anger. The authors seemed to know what I needed before I could put it into words myself. And that's the gift of this book – it doesn't just talk about grief; it walks through it with you. Quietly. Faithfully. One day at a time.

Looking back, I can honestly say this book helped me reclaim a sense of direction. It didn't rush me or promise quick healing. Instead, it whispered, *"You're not alone. You're not stuck. You're not beyond hope."* And in that season of grief, those words were like water to my soul.

How These Books Shaped My Healing Journey

These books didn't take away the pain. Nothing could. The ache of losing Cathy was too deep, too sacred to simply be erased by words on a page. But what these books did give me was something just as important: The tools to carry the pain. They offered me a language for my grief, a framework for what I was experiencing, and permission to feel the full weight of my loss without guilt or fear. They didn't ask me to rush toward resolution. They gave me space to sit with my sorrow and reminded me that doing so was not only okay – it was necessary.

What surprised me the most was how deeply personal these books became to me. They didn't feel like academic studies or distant reflections. They felt like voices beside me, walking the road with me. Each author, in their own way, reached into my experience and said, "You're not crazy. You're not alone. Others have walked this path too." And somehow, that reminder – that others had made it through – gave me the courage to believe I could as well. These books met me where I was: In the confusion, the numbness, the anger, and the longing. They helped me see that I wasn't broken – I was grieving. And grief, when faced honestly, is a reflection of how deeply we have loved.

Over time, I came to see that grief isn't something we move on from – it's something we learn to walk with. These books helped me make peace with that truth. They showed me that healing doesn't mean forgetting. It means learning how to carry both the love and the loss at the same time. That shift in perspective changed everything for me. I didn't have to deny my sadness to find strength. I could grieve and hope, mourn and trust, ache and move forward – all at the same time. That gave me freedom. And slowly, it gave me peace.

Above all, these books helped me to see something I needed more than anything: That God was still present, even in the darkness. I may not have always felt Him. There were days when I wasn't sure how to pray or even what to believe. But woven through the pages of these books was a quiet reassurance that God had not abandoned me. He was in the silence. He was in the tears. He was in the words that helped me breathe again. And through that, I began to understand something deeper than doctrine – I began to understand that God grieves with us. That He meets us in the valley and walks beside us with tenderness, patience, and love.

The Power of GriefShare: Healing in Community

Attending a 12-week GriefShare group became one of the most impactful, unexpected blessings of my entire healing journey. I still remember walking into that first session – my heart heavy, my expectations guarded. I had no idea what to expect. A part of me wondered if I even belonged there. Would this really help? Could talking to a group of strangers about something so personal and painful possibly make a difference? I wasn't sure. In fact, I almost didn't go.

But something happened in that room that changed everything. As I sat and listened, I realized I was surrounded by people who spoke the language of loss fluently. I didn't have to explain the heaviness in my chest, the exhaustion that clung to me, or the moments when tears came out of nowhere. They just understood. No judgment. No pressure. Just presence. It was the first time I felt like I could take a deep breath in the middle of my grief and not have to hide it.

What made GriefShare so powerful wasn't just the curriculum – it was people. People who had lost spouses, parents, children, siblings. People who knew the silence of an empty house, the ache of birthdays and anniversaries, the struggle to keep going when everything inside you wants to stop. And yet, there we were – showing up week after week, gently holding space for one another. We cried. We laughed. We listened. We prayed. And slowly, layer by layer, the walls came down.

GriefShare gave me more than information – it gave me companionship, validation, and hope. It reminded me that healing doesn't happen in isolation. And even though grief is incredibly personal, the journey doesn't have to be walked alone. Being part of that group reminded me of something sacred: when broken hearts come together, healing begins to multiply.

Key Lessons from GriefShare

One of the most important truths I learned in GriefShare is that grief is not linear. It doesn't follow a predictable pattern or timeline. Healing doesn't arrive in neat stages or on a schedule. Some days I felt strong. Other days I felt like I was back at the beginning. There were setbacks. Sudden waves of sorrow. Unexpected moments that took my breath away. And through it all, I learned that this was normal – not a sign of failure, but a sign of love still learning how to live with loss.

I also learned that grief can be incredibly lonely, even when you're surrounded by people. You can be in a crowd and still feel isolated, because the pain you're carrying is invisible to most. But sharing your grief with others who have walked a similar road changes that. There's healing in honesty. There's comfort in realizing you don't have to explain everything. Sometimes just saying, "Me, too," or hearing someone else say it, makes all the difference.

Another powerful lesson was about guilt and regret – those relentless *what ifs* and *if onlys* that sneak into your thoughts when you least expect them. I realized these emotions are a normal part of the grieving process. Most of us carry them in some form. But what I learned is that guilt and regret do not define our love, nor do they discredit the depth of our loss. They are visitors, not permanent residents. And through God's grace, they can be released over time.

Perhaps the most life-giving lesson of all was this: Healing doesn't mean forgetting. Moving forward with life doesn't dishonor the person we lost – it honors them. It reflects the impact they had on us. It says, "Your love made me stronger. Your memory helps me keep going." I began to understand that living again, loving again, even laughing again, are all ways of carrying their legacy forward. Healing isn't the absence of pain – it's the presence of purpose in the midst of it.

Close Friendships - A Lifeline in Grief

Grief has a way of making you feel isolated, even when you're surrounded by people who love you. It carves out a space inside you that no one else can fully enter. And while my family was my foundation during those early days, there were also a few close friends who became lifelines – steady, faithful companions who helped me hold on when the weight of sorrow threatened to pull me under. One of those friends was Dale. He and I have been close for more than 30 years. We've shared life, ministry, joys, and disappointments. And long before Cathy passed, we had established a tradition of meeting every Tuesday morning for coffee. At first, it was just friendship. Just time to catch up. But after Cathy's passing, those Tuesday mornings became something much more – they became sacred space. A quiet, familiar rhythm in the middle of the storm. A place where I could be real, raw, and unfiltered.

Every week, I sat across from someone who didn't just know me – he understood me. He didn't try to fix my pain or throw Bible verses as a bandage. He didn't give me timelines or expectations. He just listened. Some mornings, I needed to talk about Cathy. About the ache of waking up without her. About the dreams we had that would never be lived out. Other mornings, I simply needed someone to sit with me in silence. Dale always gave me that space. He never made me feel like I was too much – or not enough.

Those conversations weren't always deep or dramatic. Sometimes we'd just sip coffee, talk about sports, or laugh about something small. But behind all of it was a kind of unspoken grace – a safe place where I didn't have to pretend to be strong. I could grieve honestly. I could let the tears come if they needed to. And not once did he try to hurry me through it. He let grief take its shape – and in doing so, he gave me room to heal.

Looking back, I realize those Tuesday mornings were more than a habit. They were a weekly reminder that I wasn't alone in my sorrow. That someone saw me, checked in on me, and simply showed up. That kind of consistent friendship is rare. And in grief, it's priceless.

Through Dale – and a small circle of trusted friends – I learned something essential: Grief is too heavy to carry alone. Yes, God is with us. Yes, family is vital. But sometimes, you need one friend who will sit with you in the ashes and say, "I'm not going anywhere." For anyone walking through loss, I can't emphasize this enough: Find that one person. Someone who won't try to fix you or rush you but will walk beside you. Because grief is not a problem to be solved – it's a journey to be walked. And walking it with a friend makes all the difference.

Journaling – Processing Grief in Private

Not all grief needs to be spoken out loud. In fact, some of the deepest, most personal moments I experienced after Cathy's passing were the ones I never said to anyone – not because I didn't trust people, but because there simply weren't words that felt right to speak out loud. The sorrow was too raw, too tangled. So, I wrote them down. In the quiet of the evening or early hours of the morning, I found myself picking up a pen and turning to the blank page – not for answers, but for release.

Journaling became a powerful outlet. It was my private sanctuary, a place where I could pour out the storm inside without judgment or expectation. There were days I filled the page with memories – Cathy's laugh, the way she danced in the kitchen, the smell of her perfume, the way she made our house feel like home. Other days, I could barely form sentences – just scattered phrases, broken thoughts, or even tears falling onto the page. But every word mattered. Because in writing, I wasn't bottling up the ache – I was giving it space to breathe.

Some nights, the grief was unbearable. The loneliness pressed in like a weight on my chest, and I didn't know what to do with the pain. I'd sit in my chair with a pen and a simple notebook – no agenda, no plan – just me, my grief, and God. I would write what I couldn't say out loud. Sometimes my entries were messy, even chaotic. But it wasn't about crafting perfect words. It was about telling the truth – *my* truth – about how much I hurt, how much I missed her, and how lost I felt.

Over time, I realized journaling was doing something unexpected. First, it helped me track my healing. In the beginning, my journal entries were drenched in sorrow. But slowly, I started noticing shifts. Small glimmers. I'd write about a meaningful conversation with one of my grandkids, or a moment of peace while walking outside. A new memory would surface that brought a smile instead of tears. The grief was still there, but it was no longer the only voice on the page. Gratitude, hope, and healing began to quietly emerge.

Second, journaling became a form of prayer for me. There were many days I couldn't find the words to pray out loud. The weight of grief made it hard to ever start. But when I picked up a pen, the prayers came in ink – raw, honest, unfiltered. "God, I miss her so much." "I don't know how to do this without her. I need you to hold me tonight." These weren't polished prayers – they were soul cries. And somehow, I knew God was listening. Even when I couldn't speak, He heard every word I wrote.

Looking back, journaling became one of the most healing and sacred practices of my entire grief journey. It helped me release what I was carrying. It helped me process without pressure. And it helped me draw close to God in ways I didn't expect. For anyone walking through grief, I cannot recommend this enough: Write it down. You don't need to be a writer. You don't need to show anyone what you write. But give your emotions a place to go. Your heart deserves that space, and your healing may just begin in the quiet honesty of a blank page.

A Moment that Changed My Perspective

One night, during a GriefShare video, I heard a statement that stopped me in my tracks: "Sometimes God allows what He hates to accomplish what He loves." I remember sitting there, staring at the screen, stunned. The words echoed in my mind and settled deep in my soul. I didn't know what to do with them. I didn't even know if I believed them at first. My heart pushed back – *How could anything good come from Cathy's suffering? How could any of this pain possibly be allowed for a greater purpose?* It felt too heavy. Too personal. Too sacred to put into a theological box. But the phrase wouldn't let go of me.

Over time, I began to wrestle with it – not to dismiss the pain, but to explore whether there was a deeper layer I hadn't yet seen. As the weeks passed and I reflected more deeply, something shifted. I started to realize that while God didn't cause this loss, He wasn't absent from it either. He wasn't sitting on the sidelines, uninvolved or uncaring. No – He was still at work, even in my pain. Slowly, I noticed how He was using this season to deepen my faith, to draw me closer to my children and grandchildren, to awaken compassion in me for others who were grieving, and even to prepare me to help others find healing too.

It wasn't a quick shift. It came gradually, through prayer, through reflection, and especially through Scripture. I began to see this pattern woven throughout the Bible – the painful chapters that led to redemption, the suffering that opened the way for salvation. One of the clearest examples is Joseph. Betrayed by his own brothers, sold into slavery, unjustly imprisoned – his suffering was real, cruel, and undeserved. And yet, when he stood face-to-face with the very people who wronged him, he said: *"You meant it for evil, but God meant it for good"* (Genesis 50:20). Joseph didn't deny the pain. He didn't pretend it didn't matter. But he trusted that God was sovereign even in the suffering – and that trust changed everything.

But of course, the greatest example is Jesus. The cross – the most brutal and unjust suffering the world has ever witnessed – looked like tragedy. Jesus was mocked, beaten, pierced, and crucified. From a human perspective, it was the darkest moment in history. But from heaven's view, it was redemption unfolding. His suffering wasn't pointless. It was the very pathway to salvation. His death made way for resurrection. And because of that, we have hope beyond the grave.

Those stories reminded me that even in the devastating pain of losing Cathy, God was not absent. He was not finished. He was not wasting a single tear. I may not understand all of His purposes – and I may never fully understand them this side of heaven – but I've come to trust that He is always working for the good. Always weaving redemption into the darkest places. Always writing a bigger story than we can see in the moment. This perspective didn't take away my grief. But it gave me hope within it. It gave my suffering meaning. And that realization – that my pain wasn't meaningless, that God was still moving – became one of the most life-changing truths I've ever embraced.

So, if you're in that place – wondering if any good could possibly come from your loss – let me gently offer what I've learned: God isn't asking you to understand everything. He's asking you to trust Him. Trust that your grief matters to Him. Trust that He will bring beauty from ashes. Maybe not today. Maybe not tomorrow. But He will. Because He's done it before. And He will do it again.

Study Guide

Bible Study Helps: Reflect and Apply

Chapter Five Summary: Grief has a way of humbling us, especially when it becomes personal. My understanding of grief was transformed – not through knowledge, but through the wisdom of others who had walked this road before me. Four books became lifelines, helping me name my sorrow, reflect on my faith, and begin to heal. GriefShare offered community, truth, and hope through shared experience. Trusted friendships and journaling gave me sacred space to process the pain. And ultimately, a single statement changed everything: *Sometimes God allows what He hates to accomplish what He loves.* Through it all, I began to believe that God was not wasting my suffering – He was using it to shape something far deeper in me than I could have imagined.

Key Scriptures for Reflection

Genesis 50:20	*"But as for you, you meant evil against me; but God meant it for good…"*
Romans 8:28	*"And we know that all things work together for good to those who love God, to those who are the called according to His purpose."*
2 Corinthians 1:3–4	*"…the God of all comfort, who comforts us in all our tribulation, that we may be able to comfort those who are in any trouble…"*
Psalm 56:8	*"You number my wanderings; put my tears into Your bottle; are they not in Your book?"*
Hebrews 4:15–16	*"For we do not have a High Priest who cannot sympathize with our weaknesses … Let us therefore come boldly to the throne of grace …"*

Reflection Questions

1. Have you ever discovered unexpected wisdom or comfort through a book, message, or conversation while grieving? What did it reveal to you?
2. How have your views about grief or healing changed since your loss?
3. Are you allowing yourself to grieve in private as well as in community? What role could journaling or personal reflection play in your healing?
4. Who in your life has been a steady, listening presence during your grief journey? How has their friendship helped you?
5. Can you recall a time when God used your pain to help or comfort someone else?

Going Deeper

God doesn't waste our suffering. He walks with us through it and often uses the darkest valleys to reveal the deepest truths. Reflect on the people, books, or experiences that have become a part of your healing journey. What has God taught you through them? How is your story – your raw, unfinished, deeply human story – becoming a source of comfort and hope for others?

Prayer Prompt

Write a prayer asking God to show you how He is working in your grief, even when you can't see the full picture. Be honest about your questions, your doubts, and your longings. Ask Him to help you trust His purpose and to use your healing to bring light to someone else's darkness. *(Use the space on the next page to write your prayer.)*

_____

_____

_____

_____

_____

_____

Journal Your Thoughts

_____

_____

_____

_____

_____

_____

_____

_____

_____

_____

_____

CHAPTER 6

Finding Healing Through Serving

Finding Purpose Again: The Struggle to Say Yes

IN THE EARLY STAGES OF MY GRIEF, I was convinced I would never find purpose again. It wasn't just that I had lost Cathy – I had lost the shared mission, the rhythm of our life together, and the quiet sense of meaning that came from simply walking beside her every day. Everything in me felt emptied out. The idea of helping others seemed not only impossible – it felt almost offensive. How could I possibly pour into someone else when I was so deeply broken? When I could barely breathe through the fog of my own loss?

I didn't realize it at the time, but I had begun to believe that grief had disqualified me from being useful. That maybe for a season, or maybe forever, my role was simply to survive. I wasn't ready to give. I wasn't even sure I was ready to receive. I just wanted to make it through another day. But God, in His quiet and loving way, had other plans.

One night, just before heading to my GriefShare group, I sensed something stirring in my spirit. It wasn't loud or dramatic – just a whisper. A nudge. A sense that the Lord was saying, *"Be open. Be willing to encourage someone else tonight."* My immediate reaction was resistance. This was supposed to be my space – my time to grieve, to receive, to sit in the safety of not having to do anything for anyone. I didn't want to shift into "pastor mode." I wasn't ready to be strong.

But I couldn't shake the feeling. And so I whispered a simple, surrendered prayer – more out of obedience than confidence. *Okay, Lord. If that's what You want... I'll be open. But You'll have to lead me.* It wasn't a grand act of faith. It was more like a mustard seed. But it was real. And that quiet act of surrender became the doorway to something I never expected – healing through serving.

My First Step in Serving: Sharing About the Book That Changed My Life

That very night, something remarkable happened. As we were wrapping up the GriefShare session, one of the leaders – Leah – turned to me and said, "Dave, would you be willing to share about that book you mentioned? The one that helped you so much?" Without hesitation, I said yes. I'm still not sure why. Maybe it was the prayer I had whispered earlier. Maybe it was God's gentle way of nudging me forward. But something inside of me opened up.

For about 10 minutes, I spoke to the group about *Getting to the Other Side of Grief* – how I'd read it multiple times, how it had changed the way I saw my loss, and how it had helped me begin to heal. I wasn't trying to teach. I wasn't offering polished insights. I was just sharing honestly from my heart – as one broken person speaking to other broken hearts.

What happened next stunned me. By the end of that session, two people had already pulled out their phones and ordered the book on Amazon. Another approached me and asked the best place to find it. But it wasn't about the book, it was about connection. About realizing that my pain had the power to comfort someone else. That my story mattered – not because it was tied up in a neat bow, but because it was *real*.

That moment shifted something deep inside me. I realized that God wasn't waiting for me to be fully healed to be used. He was using the very pain I thought had sidelined me to touch others in their grief. And in that moment, something beautiful began to rise out of the ashes. *Purpose.* Not in spite of my sorrow – but through it. It was the first time I began to believe that maybe my story wasn't over. That maybe, just maybe, God still had something meaningful for me to do.

And all it took was a small yes.

A New Way to Minister: Encouraging Another Widower

That very same night, another unexpected door opened. One of the group leaders, Darrell, pulled me aside after the session. With a quiet, thoughtful tone, he said, "Dave, there's someone who could really use a conversation. He's a widower. Lost his wife several months ago. Would you be willing to talk with him?"

My first reaction was a mix of hesitation and humility. Part of me wondered, *What do I have to offer? I'm still grieving myself. I'm not a counselor. I'm not even sure I'm strong enough for this.* But another part of me remembered that small prayer I had prayed – *Okay, Lord, I'm open.* And I realized this might be God's answer to that prayer. So I said yes.

We met not long after. It wasn't formal. No polished advice. No five-step plan to navigate grief. Just two men sitting together, both broken by the same kind of loss, both learning how to breathe again. I shared what I could – what helped me, what I was still struggling with, how I had come to understand that healing didn't mean forgetting. I talked about the emotional fog, the exhaustion, the sacredness of just surviving some days. And I told him about *Getting to the Other Side of Grief*. I told him it wasn't a magic fix, but it had helped me name what I couldn't yet say out loud. He listened quietly. Nodded. And thanked me.

Months went by. Life moved forward, but that conversation stuck with me. I hadn't thought much about what kind of impact it had made. Until one day, I happened to see him at church, and he told me that he had read the book I recommended – not just once, but over and over again. Just like I had. It had become his companion, his journal, his guide. It helped him breathe, think, and grieve with hope. And for him, it was life-changing.

Just hearing that hit me deeply. Not because I had done anything extraordinary – but because in that moment, I saw something so clearly: God was using my grief to help someone else survive theirs. I didn't have to be healed to be helpful. I didn't have to be whole to be used. All I had to be was willing.

And what I discovered was this: Serving others didn't delay my healing – it deepened it. It reminded me that grief, while personal, doesn't have to be isolating. That ministry doesn't end when the title changes or the pulpit fades. Ministry is presence. It's compassion. It's sitting in the ashes with someone else and saying, "I've been there. And you're not alone."

That moment was a defining one. It gave me purpose in the pain. It reminded me that God is still writing my story, even in this new chapter.

And that maybe the most powerful way to honor Cathy – and the God we both loved – was to keep showing up, keep saying yes, and let Him use my story to breathe life into someone else's.

The Power of Community: Leading a Men's Group

One of the greatest surprises in my healing journey has been the quiet realization that people were watching me grieve. Not in a critical or intrusive way, but curiosity, reverence, and maybe even hope. My journey – raw, imperfect, and deeply personal – was impacting others in ways I never anticipated. That realization was both humbling and sacred.

Most of the men in my small group had once sat under my leadership while I was pastoring. They had seen me preach, teach, and offer guidance from the pulpit. But now, they were watching me walk through something no sermon could prepare me for: Life without Cathy. They weren't just listening to my words – they were observing my walk. And in that space, something happened. Several of the men, many of them around my same age, started opening up about their own fears and questions. For the first time, some began to process the reality that one day, they too could face a loss like mine.

Some of them told me directly, while others said it in passing – but their words stuck with me: "Dave, we're watching you. You're showing us how to grieve well." I was taken aback. I never set out to model anything. I was just doing my best to survive one day at a time. I had no grand plan, no perfect strategy. I was simply putting one foot in front of the other, trying to hold onto my faith while navigating the uncharted territory of deep sorrow. But somehow, even in my uncertainty, God was using my life as a living sermon.

That realization was overwhelming at times. I didn't want to be anyone's example. I just wanted to be honest. But the more I shared, the more the group began to open up. Our conversations deepened. The masks came off. We didn't just talk about surface-level topics – we talked about loss, aging, legacy, faith, purpose, and pain. Month after month, as I led this group, I witnessed something beautiful: men discovering that it's okay to feel, okay to question, and okay to keep trusting God even when life doesn't go as planned.

Men especially don't always have safe places to talk about these things. But this group became that place. A sacred circle where vulnerability wasn't a weakness – it was a path to healing. We laughed. We cried. We prayed. And through it all, God reminded me that community is essential to healing. I never imagined that serving others would become such a crucial part of my own restoration, but now I can say with confidence – it has been one of my greatest gifts of my journey.

Leading these men and walking with them as they walked with me reminded me that even in the midst of grief, God is still writing stories. He's still building bridges between hearts. He's still using brokenness to bring about healing – not just for me, but for others, too. And in that, I've found something I wasn't sure I'd ever find again: Purpose with joy.

Reflections on How Serving Shifted My Healing

In the beginning, I believed I had to be completely healed before I could offer anything to anyone else. I thought that helping others required strength, wholeness, and clarity – three things I didn't feel I had. Grief had stripped me down to the core. I was exhausted, heartbroken, and unsure of who I even was without Cathy by my side. The idea of serving others felt premature, even impossible. How could I pour out when I felt so empty?

Slowly, God began to change my perspective. Through small steps – sharing about a book, sitting with a fellow widower, leading a men's group – I began to see something I hadn't expected. Healing and serving weren't two separate journeys. They were intertwined. I didn't have to wait until the wound was closed to offer comfort to others. In fact, it was often in the midst of my own vulnerability that others were most encouraged. My grief didn't disqualify me – it *connected* me.

When I started focusing on helping others, something in me shifted. My grief didn't magically disappear. I still missed Cathy with every fiber of my being. There were still days when the weight of her absence took my breath away. But for the first time, I wasn't just surviving anymore. I was moving forward with purpose. Serving gave me a reason to get up in the morning. It pulled me outside of my pain and reminded me that I still had something to give – that I still had something *to live for*.

More than that, serving others helped me reclaim a piece of myself. The pastor. The encourager. The one who walks with people through their pain. That part of me hadn't died when Cathy passed – it had just gone quiet. And now, God was gently reviving it – not in the same way, but in a new, deeper way, shaped by sorrow, compassion, and wisdom that only suffering can produce. There was something sacred about realizing that God was using my brokenness, not in spite of it, but *through* it. I didn't need to have all the answers. I didn't need to pretend I was okay. I just needed to show up, share what I had, and let God do the rest. And every time I did, I felt a little more alive. A little more anchored. A little more like myself again.

I now believe with all my heart that serving others while grieving is not a sign of strength – it's a pathway to healing. When we offer our pain to God, He has a way of turning it into purpose. And in doing so, He doesn't just work through us – He works in us.

The Biblical Foundation of Serving Through Pain

One of the most powerful revelations in my healing journey was realizing that the call to serve doesn't wait for the pain to pass. It begins right in the heart of it. And this truth isn't just something I stumbled upon – it's deeply biblical. The scriptures are filled with examples of people who served others not after their suffering was over, but in the very middle of it.

Look at Jesus. On the night before His crucifixion, when the weight of the world's sin was already pressing on His shoulders, when He was about to endure betrayal, agony, and the cross – He knelt down and washed His disciples' feet. He served with humility and love in His moment of deepest sorrow. He didn't withdraw. He leaned in. His grief didn't stop His compassion – it magnified it.

Paul, in 2 Corinthians 1:3–4, echoes this same truth: *"Blessed be the God … who comforts us in all our tribulation, that we may be able to comfort those who are in any trouble …"* Paul makes it clear – our comfort is never meant to end with us. It's meant to flow through us. God meets us in our grief not just to heal us, but to equip us to bring healing to others.

And then there's Isaiah 61:1–3 – a passage I've come to treasure. It declares that God binds up the brokenhearted, gives beauty for ashes, the oil of joy for mourning, the garment of praise for the spirit of heaviness. This is not poetic metaphor – it's a promise. Grief does not get the final word. God does. And He specializes in taking what feels shattered and shaping it into something redemptive. Not by removing our pain, but by redeeming it – using it as a vessel to carry His love into the lives of others.

The Bible doesn't ask us to be perfect or pain-free before we serve. It simply invites us to bring our whole selves – wounded, weary, but willing – and trust that God will do what only He can: Take what was meant for sorrow and use it for strength, both in our lives and in the lives of those we touch.

Encouragement for Those Who Feel Like They'll Never Have Purpose Again

If you're reading this today and you're in the middle of deep grief – and the idea of ever finding purpose again feels impossible – please hear me: I understand. I really do. I've been there. I know what it's like to stare at the ceiling, wondering how you'll get through another day. I know the emptiness that comes from losing someone you love so deeply that your entire identity feels torn apart. I've sat in the silence and thought, *Is this it now? Just surviving?*

For a long time, I couldn't imagine doing anything beyond just existing. The idea of helping someone else felt completely out of reach. I was the one who needed help. I was the one broken and worn down. But what I've learned – what has completely reshaped my view of grief – is this: purpose doesn't arrive after the pain is over. It begins *in the middle of it*, when we dare to open our hearts, even just a little, and say, "God, if You can use this, I'm willing."

I thought I had to be healed before I could serve. But the moment I said yes – even just a quiet, uncertain yes – something changed. When I shared about *Getting to the Other Side of Grief* that night in GriefShare, I realized that my pain had the power to help someone else. When I sat across from another widower, I saw in his eyes the same fog I had once walked through – and I knew my story could be a light for his path. When I led the men's group and saw how others were watching me grieve, it became clear: My life, even in its brokenness, was offering strength to others.

And here's what I want you to know: You don't have to feel ready. You don't have to have all the answers. You don't need to feel strong or prepared or certain. God isn't looking for perfection – He's simply asking for openness. Be open to encouraging just one person. Be open to sharing even one sentence of your story. Be open to the idea that your deepest sorrow might one day become someone else's survival.

Because here's the beautiful, unexpected truth: when you let God use your story, healing doesn't just flow to others – it flows back to you. Every time you give a piece of your pain to someone who needs hope, God gently fills that space in your heart with grace, strength, and yes – purpose. You are not done. Your life still matters. Your grief has not rendered you useless – it has made you tender, empathetic, and real in a way the world desperately needs. And the God who brought beauty from ashes then, is doing it in you even now.

Study Guide

Bible Study Helps: Reflect and Apply

Chapter Six Summary: In this chapter, I share how serving others became a surprising and essential part of my healing journey. In the beginning, I didn't think I had anything to give – I was the one broken by grief. Over time, I discovered that God wasn't waiting for me to be fully healed before using me. Whether it was sharing a book in GriefShare, sitting with another widower, or leading a men's group, I saw how God used my pain as a bridge to connect with others. Serving didn't take away my grief, but it gave it purpose. I came to understand that healing and helping aren't separate paths – they often grow side by side. And through it all, God reminded me that I wasn't disqualified by my sorrow – I was being shaped by it to bring comfort and hope to others.

Key Scriptures for Reflection

2 Corinthians 1:3–4	*"Blessed be the God … who comforts us in all our tribulation, that we may be able to comfort those who are in any trouble …"*
John 13:14–15	*"If then, your Lord and Teacher, have washed your feet, you also ought to wash one another's feet."*
Isaiah 61:3	*"… to give them beauty for ashes, the oil of joy for mourning, the garment of praise for the spirit of heaviness …"*
Romans 12:11–12	*"… fervent in spirit, serving the Lord; rejoicing in hope, patient in tribulation, continuing steadfastly in prayer."*
Galatians 6:2	*"Bear one another's burdens, and so fulfill the law of Christ."*

Reflection Questions

1. What fears or doubts have kept you from believing God could still use you in this season of grief?
2. Has there been a moment when sharing your story or encouraging someone else brought unexpected comfort to your own heart?
3. What does it look like to serve others without being "fully healed"? How does the idea challenge or encourage you?
4. Can you think of someone who had walked beside you in your grief? What did their presence mean to you?
5. In what ways might God be gently inviting you to serve, even if it's just in small, quiet ways?
6. Which of the key scriptures spoke most deeply to you? Why?

Going Deeper

Serving others while grieving may feel counterintuitive – but it can become one of the most healing steps we take. When we offer our brokenness to God, He doesn't discard it – He redeems it. Take some time to reflect on the areas of your life where God might want to use your story, your experiences, and your pain to encourage someone else. It doesn't need to be public. It just needs to be offered.

Prayer Prompt

Write a prayer asking God to show you where and how He might want to use your grief for good. Be honest about your hesitations, and ask Him to give you a willing, open heart. Surrender your story to Him and trust that He is not finished writing it. *(Use the space on the next page to write your prayer.)*

_____

_____

_____

_____

_____

_____

_____

Journal Your Thoughts

_____

_____

_____

_____

_____

_____

_____

_____

_____

_____

_____

_____

CHAPTER 7

Faith and Grief -
Wrestling with God

Faith After Loss: Not a Crisis, But a Shift

I DIDN'T HAVE A CRISIS OF FAITH AFTER CATHY PASSED – but I can honestly say I'll never look at the promises of Scripture the same way again. Before Cathy's death, faith meant declaring and standing on God's Word with unwavering trust. I had fasted, prayed, and spoken every healing verse I knew over her life. I believed in miracles. I had witnessed them before. I was holding on with everything in me for one more. I thought that if I just believed hard enough, confessed long enough, and prayed faithfully enough, God would surely heal her.

But when Cathy died, it altered something at my core. My faith didn't break – but it was reshaped. I realized that the promises of God are always true, but the way He fulfills them is often different than we expect. Healing didn't come the way I asked – but it came in a deeper, eternal form. I now see that God's purpose determines the time and the method. And His purpose is always greater than mine. That truth was hard to swallow at first – especially after years in ministry, watching more prayers for healing go unanswered than answered. But it wasn't until the loss was my own that I had to wrestle with it on a soul-deep level.

Faith, for me, has become less about getting the outcome I want and more about trusting God's heart even when I don't understand His hand. It's not that I've stopped believing for miracles – I haven't. It's that I now carry a humility with that belief. I understand that true faith isn't proven by results – it's proven by surrender. It's the kind of faith that says, "Even if He doesn't, I will still trust Him." That's the kind of faith I've been learning to live with since Cathy went to heaven. Not one built on formulas or expectations, but on the unshakable truth that God is still good, even when life isn't.

The Deep Questions I Asked God

Grief brings questions – and I had plenty. In the days and weeks after Cathy's passing, I found myself wrestling with thoughts that kept circling, unrelenting. These weren't theological puzzles or abstract reflections. They were gut-level cries from a broken heart. *Why now?* We had just moved into our brand-new custom home – something we had prayed and planned for over many years. The home was beautiful, filled with sunlight and space for family memories. It was supposed to be the place where we enjoyed our next season of life together. And yet, Cathy never truly got to enjoy it. Just a year and eight months after moving in, she was gone. Why?

Why her? Of all people, why Cathy? She was the kindest, gentlest, most selfless woman I have ever known. Everyone loved her – and I truly mean that. Her Celebration of Life service in the middle of summer brought over 600 people. That wasn't just a reflection of her impact. It was a testimony of the quiet, steady love she poured into others. *Why would God take someone like that?*

I found myself asking: *Why did she have to suffer the entire time we lived in our new home? Why did the cancer have to spread so fast, so relentlessly? Why all the treatments, the blood draws, the chemo – the hope we tried to hold onto – if You were going to take her anyway?* These weren't questions rooted in rebellion. They came from a place of longing. A desperate desire to understand. To make sense of the senseless. I poured out my heart to God – not in anger, but in grief, in longing, in aching love.

There were no easy answers. In fact, there were no answers at all – just silence. And in that silence, I was faced with a choice: Would I still trust God even when I didn't get the answers I wanted? Would I believe He was good, even when life felt unbearably cruel? Would I surrender my need to understand in exchange for deeper dependence on His presence? That became the true wrestling match – not between me and God's promises, but between me and my need for control.

Grief doesn't just change your emotions. It challenges your theology. It forces you to look at faith not as a series of beliefs, but as a relationship built on trust. And in those quiet hours – often in the middle of the night, sitting alone in a chair with tears running down my face – I began to discover that faith isn't the absence of questions. It's choosing to stay in the conversation with God even when the answers don't come.

Biblical Examples: When Others Wrestled with God

Job - Questioning Without Losing Faith

Job's story is one of the most honest portraits of human suffering in all of Scripture. He lost everything – his children, his wealth, his health – yet he never cursed God. That doesn't mean he didn't wrestle. In fact, Job's questions were some of the most raw and desperate ever recorded. *"Why was I ever born?" "Why do You hide Your face and consider me Your enemy?"* He poured out his heart without restraint. He was confused, angry, broken – but still faithful. Job didn't pretend to be okay, and God didn't punish him for asking. He allowed the questions. He welcomed the lament.

What's most striking is that God never gave Job all the answers he was seeking. He didn't explain the why behind every tragedy. Instead, God revealed something deeper – His sovereignty, His power, and His presence. He reminded Job that some things are simply beyond human understanding. Job's story has become an anchor for me. It reminds me that it's okay to ask questions without losing faith. That God can handle my grief, my confusion, even my frustration. Job never stopped engaging with God, and that's what faith looks like: Staying in the conversation, even through the storm.

There have been days I've asked my own version of Job's questions. *Why did this happen? Where are You in this?* And I've come to realize what Job did – that sometimes, peace doesn't come from having answers. It comes from knowing that God is still God, and He is still with me. That is often enough.

David - Grief and Worship Co-Existing

David was called a man after God's own heart, but he was also a man of deep, unfiltered emotion. His psalms are full of lament, doubt, sorrow, and fear. David didn't hide his grief – he brought it into the presence of God. *"How long, O Lord? Will You forget me forever?"* He asked hard questions, but he never let go of worship. That's what moves me most about David's example: Grief and trust lived side by side. He didn't wait until everything was okay to lift his voice in praise. He trusted in the dark. He praised through tears.

I resonate deeply with David's journey. There were days when I could barely breathe from the weight of sorrow. And yet – even in that heaviness – I found myself whispering prayers of gratitude, declarations of trust. Sometimes, just saying, "Lord, I still believe You're good," felt like the most courageous act I could muster. Like David, I've discovered that grief and worship don't cancel each other out. They can co-exist. One doesn't have to wait for the other to be resolved.

David teaches us that God doesn't need polished prayers. He wants honesty. He wants us to show up with what we have – even if all we have is pain. Wrestling with God doesn't mean walking away from Him. It means leaning into Him with everything we've got – even our brokenness. And I've found that in doing that, healing begins.

Jesus - The Ultimate Wrestling in Gethsemane

And then there's Jesus. The Son of God – the One who knew the full plan of redemption, the One who walked in perfect obedience – still wrestled with suffering. In the Garden of Gethsemane, just hours before His arrest, Jesus prayed, *"Father, if You are willing, take this cup from Me."* That single sentence reveals the depth of His anguish. Jesus knew the pain ahead – emotional, physical, and spiritual. And in His humanity, He struggled. He wept. He asked if there was another way.

But what came next is what has shaped my grief more than anything else: *"Yet not My will, but Yours be done."* Jesus surrendered – not because the pain didn't matter, but because the purpose of God was greater. That's what I've had to learn. I prayed for Cathy's healing. I begged God for a miracle. I fasted, I believed. And yet, God called her home. And I had to choose, just like Jesus did, to surrender.

This moment in Gethsemane reminds me that it's not unspiritual to wrestle. It's Christlike. Wrestling is not rebellion – it's relationship. Jesus wrestled, and then He trusted. That has become the model for me. In the depths of my grief, I can still say, *"Not my will, but Yours be done."* It doesn't erase the pain, but it anchors me in a deeper truth: God's purpose being fulfilled, even when I don't understand it.

What Ultimately Strengthened My Faith - Trusting in God's Purpose

I came to realize something that transformed my entire perspective on faith: God's faithfulness is not measured by how often He answers my prayers the way I want. For most of my life, I subconsciously equated God's goodness with answered prayers, protection from pain, and miracles that aligned with my hopes. I believed in a God who did the impossible – and I still do. But when Cathy died, I had to ask myself: *Is God still faithful even when the outcome breaks your heart?*

It was not an easy conclusion to reach, but it was a necessary one. God's faithfulness isn't based on the result – it's rooted in His character. He is faithful because He is present. Because He sustains. Because He walks with us through the valley, not just around it. The more I leaned into that truth, the more I found peace. Not because the grief was gone, but because I started seeing God's goodness in the midst of it. Not just in spite of it. Over time, I began to understand that God's purpose is bigger than my understanding. There are layers to His will that I will never comprehend this side of eternity. And while I still wrestle with the *why*, I no longer let it dictate my faith. I've learned to live with mystery, to sit with the unanswered, and to trust that what I can't see is still being held together by the hands of a loving Father.

It's a humbling thing to admit, especially after decades in ministry. I used to preach about God's plan with boldness and confidence – and I still do. But now I speak it through the ache of personal loss, knowing firsthand that His plan sometimes includes heartbreak. Faith, to me, has become less about declarations and more about surrender. Less about control, and more about trust. It's no longer a belief system I stand on –

it's a relationship I fall into.

And here's what I've come to know: When I don't understand His plan, I can still trust His heart. That truth has carried me through the hardest season of my life. Cathy's passing didn't shake my faith. It refined it. It deepened it. It exposed what was built on sand and strengthened what was built on the Rock. And in the end, what remains is this: God is still good. God is still near. And God still has a purpose – even this.

Leaning into Scripture

Before Cathy's passing, I read Scripture with a certain kind of expectancy. I viewed the Word of God through the lens of claiming promises, declaring victory, believing for breakthrough. And I still believe God's Word is alive, powerful, and full of promises we can stand on. But after her death, something changed. I could no longer read Scripture as a formula for desired outcomes. It wasn't about claiming healing or predicting answers. It became something else entirely – a guide for the valley, a source of wisdom when nothing made sense, and a steady voice when all others grew quiet.

In those early days of grief, I searched the Scriptures not for answers, but for something to hold on to – something that could walk with me through the unknown. I realized something I hadn't really admitted before: No matter how much Scripture I knew, it didn't answer my *why* questions. It didn't explain the timing, the suffering, the silence. But it did something even more important– it provided direction. It offered strength when I was empty. It reminded me that I wasn't walking through grief alone. God was still speaking. He was still leading me, one step at a time. One verse that brought unexpected clarity was Ecclesiastes 7:14: *"In the day of prosperity be joyful, but in the day of adversity consider: surely God has appointed one as well as the other."* That verse confronted me in a way I wasn't prepared for. It reminded me that God isn't just present in the blessings – He's sovereign over the sorrow, too. It's a humbling and anchoring truth. God is the author of every season. The ones we long for and the ones we never would have chosen. That didn't take away my pain, but it did remind me that my pain wasn't outside of His reach. He hadn't turned away. He was walking with me through it.

Even with that, I struggled to reconcile Cathy's suffering. I found myself wrestling not just with her death, but with the journey that led to it. The long months of treatments, the slow decline, the moments of hope that slipped through our fingers. And then I came back to Isaiah 55:8–9: *"'For My thoughts are not your thoughts, nor are your ways My ways,' says the Lord. 'For as the heavens are higher than the earth, so are My ways higher than your ways, and My thoughts than your thoughts.'"* I had read that verse countless times, but now it spoke differently. It wasn't a vague idea – it was a compassionate boundary. A reminder that I am not God, and I don't have to understand everything to trust Him.

That verse didn't silence my questions – but it gave me peace in the absence of answers. Faith is not about figuring everything out – it's about resting in the character of the One who already has.

As I continued to lean into Scripture, I found it didn't remove my grief, but it reframed it. It didn't explain the pain, but it gave me language for it. More than anything, it reminded me that when the path ahead is unclear, God is still lighting the way – one verse, one promise, one quiet assurance at a time.

Conversations with Family - Processing Faith Together

One of the unexpected gifts in my grief journey was the depth of the conversations I had with my family – not just about memories or emotions, but about faith itself. In the weeks and months after Cathy passed, we didn't avoid the hard questions. We leaned into them. We sat around kitchen tables, walked together, shared texts and phone calls – and in those spaces, we wrestled through our beliefs, not apart from one another, but together.

There were no easy answers. Sometimes we just sat in silence, acknowledging the ache. Other times, we cried together and asked the questions that live at the edge of grief: *Why now? Why this way? Where was God in all of this?* And yet, in those raw conversations, I realized something beautiful: My faith wasn't becoming weaker. It was being refined in community.

These weren't theological debates or forced pep talks. They were holy moments of honesty. I didn't pretend to have all the answers – not as a pastor, not as a father, not as a Papa. But I was willing to walk with my family in the questions, and in doing so, we grew closer not only to each other, but to God. We shared Scriptures, challenged each other's assumptions, and reminded one another that faith doesn't mean bypassing grief – it means bringing our grief into God's presence, side by side.

There were times when one of my grandchildren would say something that would stop me in my tracks – words that carried wisdom beyond their years, or a perspective I hadn't considered. These moments didn't just help me lead – they helped me learn. I saw the strength of Cathy's legacy in them. I saw how her faith was still alive in their hearts. And I saw how processing faith as a family created space for healing that none of us could have found alone.

I look back at those conversations now with deep gratitude. They were reminders that while grief is personal, faith is something we're meant to carry in community. And when we carry it together, even the heaviest burdens feel just a little lighter.

Rooted in Love

There came a moment, not long after Cathy passed, when I intentionally withdrew to be alone with God. I wasn't trying to prepare a message or sort through logistics. I simply needed to sit in his presence. My heart was aching. My thoughts were tangled with grief, and though I had walked with God for decades, this loss left me disoriented in ways I had never known before. I went into that time of prayer not looking for answers as much as I was longing for clarity – something to hold onto when everything else felt shaken.

As I poured out my heart, I found myself asking God a question I had wrestled with silently for weeks: *Lord, I just need to understand… even a little.* And then – quietly, unexpectedly, and with a depth that pierced through the weight of sorrow – I sensed Him speaking something to my heart: *"The way I view you, the way I speak to you, and the way I ultimately respond to you will always be rooted in love – because I cannot act outside My character."* I sat still, overcome. It wasn't a thunderous revelation. It was more like a holy stillness, a whisper that reached a place in me deeper than my grief. That moment didn't remove the pain I was feeling, but it changed how I carried it. It reframed everything. I began to see that even when I couldn't trace God's hand, I could still trust His heart. And His heart was love – not circumstantial, not earned, not withdrawn in suffering – steadfast, eternal love.

That encounter became a spiritual stronghold. I wasn't going to receive all the answers I wanted, but I was given something even better: the assurance that nothing God allows or withholds in my life is ever outside the boundaries of His perfect love. That became enough. Even in the ache, I could rest in the reality that the One who holds me cannot act outside of His goodness.

Since that day, I've carried those words like a flame in the dark: *rooted in love*. They remind me that faith is not about figuring everything out. It's about returning again and again to the One whose very nature is love – and knowing that no matter what I face, He is not finished with my story.

Study Guide

Bible Study Helps: Reflect and Apply

Chapter Seven Summary: In this chapter, I opened up about the internal struggle that followed Cathy's passing – not a crisis of faith, but a shift. I wrestled with unanswered questions, the mystery of suffering, and how to hold on to God's promises when life turns upside down. Through prayer, Scripture, and honest conversations with my family, I discovered that God's love is still present in the unknown, and His character can be trusted even when His ways are beyond my understanding.

Key Scriptures for Reflection

Ecclesiastes 7:14	*"In the day of prosperity be joyful, but in the day of adversity consider: surely God has appointed one as well as the other…"*
Isaiah 55:8–9	*"For My thoughts are not your thoughts, nor are your ways My ways …"*
2 Corinthians 1:3–4	*"…the God of all comfort, who comforts us in all our tribulation, that we may be able to comfort those who are in any trouble…"*
Job 1:21	*"The LORD gave, and the LORD has taken away; blessed be the name of the LORD."*
Psalm 13:1–2, 5	*"How long, O LORD? Will You forget me forever? But I have trusted in Your mercy."*
Luke 22:42	*"Father, if You are willing, take this cup from Me; yet not My will, but Yours be done."*

Reflection Questions

1. Have you ever experienced a season where your understanding of faith was challenged? What did that season teach you about God?
2. What questions have you wrestled with in grief that remain unanswered? How do you handle that tension?
3. How do you personally respond when Scripture doesn't give you the clarity you're seeking? What do you do next?
4. What does trusting God's character look like for you in seasons of uncertainty or loss?
5. Have you ever had a moment when God spoke clearly to your heart in grief? What did He reveal to you?

Going Deeper

Sometimes the most honest thing we can do in our grief is ask the hard questions. God isn't offended by your wrestling. In fact, He invites it. When we bring our doubt, confusion, and heartache into His presence, we create space for deeper trust – not based on outcome but based on who He is. Revisit a Scripture that once brought you comfort and read it through the lens of your current season. What fresh truth is God revealing now?

Prayer Prompt

Spend a few moments in quiet reflection. Write a prayer to God that doesn't hold anything back – your questions, frustrations, fears, and hopes. Let it be honest. Let it be raw. Then ask Him to help you trust not just in what He does, but in who He is. *(Use the space on the next page to write your prayer.)*

Journal Your Thoughts

CHAPTER 8

Hope Beyond the Horizon

The Unimaginable Possibility of Happiness

IN THE EARLIEST DAYS OF GRIEF, HAPPINESS FELT LIKE A FOREIGN CONCEPT – something that belonged to another life, a life that ended the day Cathy took her final breath. In those first few weeks, I wasn't looking for joy. I was trying to survive. The thought of smiling again, laughing again, or feeling lightness in my spirit felt not only impossible, but almost inappropriate. How could I ever imagine happiness when the person I had loved for over five decades was no longer by my side?

But over time, I began to realize something surprising. Healing doesn't arrive all at once – but neither does hope. It comes in small glimpses, unexpected moments, and quiet realizations that life still holds meaning. I had to learn that hope is not a feeling we stumble into – it's something we begin to build. One decision at a time. One step at a time. Whether it was going to dinner with grandkids, sharing a story about Cathy, or simply getting out of bed on a hard morning, those choices began to quietly lay the foundation for something new. Not a replacement for what I had lost, but a continuation of the life I still had to live.

One of the most important things I've come to understand is that grief is not passive. It asks something of us. The authors of *Getting to the Other Side of Grief* put it best: "Grieving is an active and intentional process that takes a lot of work along with time to end up in a healthy place, which we call the other side of grief." That sentence has stayed with me. There is another side. And even though the journey is long and often painful, there is more ahead than sorrow. There is beauty. There is purpose. There is happiness. And yes – there is hope, just beyond the horizon.

Difficult Choices that Led to Healing

As I continued navigating life without Cathy, I found that grief wasn't just emotional – it came with choices. Decisions I never imagined I'd have to make. Some were practical. Others were deeply symbolic. One of the most difficult of all was deciding when – and if – I should remove my wedding ring. For over fifty years, that ring never left my finger. It was a physical reminder of a covenant I had made, a love I had cherished, a life we had built together. It symbolized loyalty, intimacy, and shared history. Taking it off felt like taking a part of Cathy away. I wrestled with the thought for months. Was it too soon? Would people misunderstand? Would I feel like I was letting go of Cathy?

It was my son Jeff who finally helped me see it from a new perspective. He gently said, "Dad, why would you keep wearing a ring that no longer symbolizes what it once did? You kept your vows. You loved her well. You walked with her to the very end. No one questions that." And then, in one of the most healing conversations I've had, all my children came alongside me and said, "Dad, you don't have to keep wearing that ring to prove anything to anyone. We saw your love. We saw your faithfulness. We support you as you move forward – whatever that looks like." Their words meant more than they probably know. It wasn't just about the ring – it was about permission. Permission to step forward without guilt. Permission to believe that my story wasn't over. Permission to carry Cathy's love with me while also remaining open to the future God may still have for me.

The authors of *Getting to the Other Side of Grief* speak to this very issue in a way that resonated deeply with me. They write,

> As you move forward toward your new volume in life, you need to address the issue of wearing your wedding ring. The ring is a powerful symbol of a time gone by, a valued reminder of memories of your former marriage, a prior volume in your life. There is no right time to remove your wedding ring, but if you are planning to move forward toward a new phase in life, it is something that does need to be done.

Reading those words affirmed what my heart already sensed: This was part of the process. Not betrayal, not an erasure of the past – but a sacred step forward.

Removing that ring wasn't easy. It was one of the most emotional things I've done. But in that moment, I realized something: Healing often requires hard, intentional choices. And sometimes, those choices don't mean forgetting or moving on. They mean honoring what was, while making room for what could be. That moment reminded me that grief and hope *can* coexist. And that my life – even in its new form – is still unfolding under the careful, loving hand of God.

Living with Gratitude Instead of Regret

One of the greatest sources of peace in my life right now is this truth: Cathy and I lived with no regrets. We said the things that mattered. We showed up for each other, again and again. We made time for laughter, even in the hard seasons. And when life threw challenges our way, we faced them together. That knowledge – that we truly cherished the years that God gave us – has become a deep well of comfort in the aftermath of loss.

We used to talk often about how blessed we were. It wasn't just surface-level gratitude. It was a deep, soul-level awareness that what we had was rare and beautiful. Three children who loved and honored us. Ten incredible grandchildren who filled our home with laughter and energy. And now, two great-grandchildren – each a living legacy of the love we started all those years ago. We didn't just build a home – we built a family. And that gave our lives richness beyond anything we could have planned.

Of course, there are moments I wish we'd had more time – more anniversaries, more travels, more quiet mornings drinking coffee together. But when I look back, I don't see a life cut short. I see a life well-lived, one full of shared purpose, quiet joy, and enduring love. That's a gift not everyone gets, and I don't take it for granted for a single moment.

Even now, as I walk forward without Cathy by my side, I do so with a heart deeply rooted in thankfulness. Gratitude continues to shape my perspective, especially on the hardest days. I can't change the fact that she's gone, but I can choose how I live in light of the love we shared. I choose to honor our marriage by continuing to live with fullness, to love with intention, and to carry her legacy forward in the way I treat others. It's not always easy – but it's always worth it.

Small Glimpses of Hope Returning

Hope doesn't return all at once. It comes gently, quietly – more like a whisper than a shout. In the early days of grief, I didn't go looking for hope. I didn't even know where to begin. But slowly, like sunlight breaking through the storm clouds, it started to find me. Not in dramatic moments, but in ordinary ones. Small, almost imperceptible glimpses of something brighter.

I remember the first time I laughed again – *really* laughed. It caught me off guard. I don't even remember what the joke was, only that for a split second, I felt light again. It was like my soul exhaled after holding its breath for far too long. Then came the dinners with my grandkids. Sitting around the table, sharing stories, hearing them say, "I love you, Papa," or asking questions about Cathy and our life together. They weren't trying to fix anything – they were just showing up. And their presence became a healing balm I didn't know I needed.

There were phone calls with my son Jeff that turned into hour-long conversations about grief, faith, and what it means to keep going when your heart feels shattered. There were early morning coffees with my friend Dale, where sometimes no words were spoken, but the silence itself was sacred. Hope showed up in those quiet Tuesday mornings, too.

Helping my children in YWAM as they serve in missions also stirred something in me. When they texted asking for prayer or called to share what God was doing in their lives, it reminded me that I still have a voice that matters, a heart that can invest in the future. My purpose didn't die with Cathy – it shifted. And part of that shift was realizing that I still have a role to play in the story God is writing in the lives of those I love.

Even leading communion at my church or speaking at my granddaughter's high school, hope kept showing up in new forms. Not as a dramatic comeback, but as a quiet reassurance: *You're still here. God's not done. There's more ahead.*

Each of these moments – so simple, so easy to overlook – became stepping stones. They reminded me that life wasn't over. It was just different. And in that difference, there was still something beautiful. There was still something worth showing up for. There was still hope.

The Surrender that Brought True Hope

The more I learned to surrender my future to God, the more hope began to quietly take root in my heart. Not the kind of hope that arrives with fanfare or dramatic answers, but a grounded, steady kind – the kind that comes when you stop trying to fix everything and start trusting the One who holds them all.

In the beginning, I wanted answers. I wanted clarity. I wanted to understand why Cathy had to suffer, why our plans were cut short, why my prayers for healing had gone unanswered. I thought that if I could just make sense of it all, then maybe I could find peace. But grief doesn't offer easy explanations. And I discovered that chasing answers often only deepened the ache.

What changed everything was surrender – not a one-time event, but a posture I had to choose daily. Surrendering meant opening my hands and letting go of the life I thought I'd still be living. It meant laying down my timeline, my expectations, and even my fears about the future. And in that surrender, something unexpected happened. I didn't feel weaker. I felt held.

I realized that hope isn't rooted in understanding – it's rooted in trust. I didn't have to know how everything would work out. I just needed to trust that God was still writing the story. And as I did, I started noticing the subtle ways He was at work – rebuilding, restoring, and repurposing the pain I carried.

There were divine appointments – conversations I never planned, moments of clarity in prayer, unexpected opportunities to speak into someone else's life. These weren't coincidences. They were reminders that even when I couldn't see the full picture, God was already at work behind the scenes.

True hope didn't come when I had everything figured out. It came when I finally admitted that I didn't. And that's when God gently reminded me: *You don't have to know the way forward. You just need to trust the One who does.*

What I've Learned About Hope Beyond Grief

Hope isn't about replacing what was lost. That's not how grief works. There is no moving on from the kind of love Cathy and I shared. There is no substitute for decades of laughter, shared dreams, parenting our children, or holding our grandkids together. Real hope doesn't ask you to forget. It invites you to remember – with gratitude – and still believe there's more ahead. That's what I've learned in this journey. Hope doesn't compete with loss; it gently rises from within it.

I used to think that grief and joy couldn't coexist. That if I was smiling again, laughing again, planning again, it meant I was dishonoring the love I had lost. But now I see that *grieving well* isn't about staying stuck in sorrow. It's about honoring your loss by allowing it to shape how you live moving forward. Grief carved out new depths in me. And those very places became the soil where hope could grow.

I've also learned that hope is not passive. It doesn't simply show up one day unannounced. Hope is a choice. A discipline. A daily, intentional decision to open your heart again. To wake up and say, "Today, I will trust that God's not finished with my story." There were mornings I didn't feel that kind of resolve. But with time, I began to realize that even the smallest acts – getting out of bed, going for a walk, picking up the phone to call a friend – were signs that hope was beginning to take root.

Hope doesn't mean the pain disappears. Even now, there are moments when the ache of Cathy's absence takes me by surprise. A smell. A song. A memory that catches me off guard. But I don't fear those moments anymore. I welcome them as reminders of a love that was real and beautiful. And because that love was real, I can walk forward with confidence that love and life remain.

There is life beyond the grief – not instead of it, but alongside it. And that life can be meaningful, rich and purposeful. I've discovered that hope makes room for both sorrow and joy. It gives you permission to hold onto what was and reach for what's next at the same time. That's the kind of hope I'm talking about. Not false positivity. Not pretending to be okay. But a quiet, steady belief that beauty can still come from brokenness.

To anyone wondering if they'll ever feel alive again, let me assure you: It's possible. Not overnight. Not without intentional effort. But if you stay open – if you keep walking – hope will come. Maybe not as a flood, but as a whisper, a flicker, a breath of fresh air you didn't expect. It comes when you serve someone else. When you laugh with your grandkids. When you remember your loved one with a smile instead of weeping. It comes when you realize that honoring your grief also means embracing your future.

When you grieve well, you *can* truly live well. Not in spite of your sorrow – but *through* it, beyond it, and even because of it. Grief has changed me, yes. But it has also refined me. It's deepened my empathy,

expanded my faith, and taught me the beauty of a hope that holds fast –
even when the horizon is far off. That's the kind of hope that lasts. And
it's available to all of us.

Study Guide

Bible Study Helps: Reflect and Apply

Chapter Eight Summary: Grief does not mark the end of your story – it reshapes it. In this chapter, I shared how hope returned gradually through difficult choices, small moments of joy, and deep surrender to God's plan. I learned that true hope is not about replacing what was lost but embracing what still lies ahead. Grieving well doesn't mean forgetting. It means honoring the past while choosing to live with intention and faith in what's still possible. Hope is built – not found – through trust, surrender, and daily choices to keep moving forward.

Key Scriptures for Reflection

Romans 15:13	*"Now may the God of hope fill you with all joy and peace in believing, that you may abound in hope by the power of the Holy Spirit."*
Isaiah 61:3	*"To console those who mourn in Zion, to give them beauty for ashes, the oil of joy for mourning, the garment of praise for the spirit of heaviness..."*
Psalm 30:5	*"Weeping may endure for a night, but joy comes in the morning."*

Reflection Questions

1. What has been the most difficult part of embracing hope after your loss?
2. Can you identify a small moment where you sensed hope returning? What did it feel like?
3. How have your views on grief and healing changed since the early days of loss?
4. What specific choice (s) have you made that helped move you toward hope again?

5. Are there moments or people in your life right now that remind you you're not alone?
6. What do you think God is inviting you to surrender as you move forward in hope?
7. In what ways has grief reshaped your understanding of what it means to live well?

Going Deeper

Read Romans 15:13 slowly, multiple times. Reflect on what it means to *"abound in hope by the power of the Holy Spirit."* This is not about forcing yourself to be okay – it's about inviting the Spirit of God into your pain, into your questions, and into your future. What would it look like to live with an open heart, trusting that hope isn't something you have to create, but something God will build within you?

Prayer Prompt

God, I'm learning that hope doesn't come all at once. It comes in the quiet, in the little moments, and in the courage to keep showing up. Help me surrender the future I imagined and trust that You are still writing a beautiful story with my life. Fill me with the kind of hope that anchors me – not because everything makes sense, but because I know You are with me. Teach me to live well, even in the presence of grief. I trust You. Amen. *(Use the space on the next page to write your prayer.)*

Journal Your Thoughts

CHAPTER 9

Living with Purpose After Loss

The Power of Saying YES

IN THE BEGINNING, SAYING YES TO ANYTHING FELT LIKE A RISK. In the early days of grief, I hesitated, unsure of whether I had anything left to offer. But as time went on, I discovered something deeper – that saying yes wasn't just about obedience in the moment – it was about embracing a new way of living. It was about stepping into life again, even while carrying the weight of loss.

Now, further along in my journey, that simple yes has grown roots. It's no longer just a response to invitations – it's a mindset of availability. A posture of the heart that says, "Lord, whatever You have for me in this season, I'm open." I've learned that this kind of yes isn't born from having all the answers. It's born from trust. From the belief that purpose still exists – not in spite of my loss, but because God is still writing something beautiful through it.

This yes has led me into rooms I never expected, into conversations I never planned, and into moments where I've felt the unmistakable presence of God at work – through my story, through my pain, through my willingness to show up. And more than that, it's restored my sense of calling. Not the same calling I had before Cathy passed, but a new one. A calling shaped by compassion, humility, and the quiet conviction that God still has more for me to do.

The power of saying yes isn't in the size of the task – it's in the surrender. It's trusting that God can do something meaningful even through small acts of faith. And over time, those small yeses begin to build something lasting: A life that's still full of purpose, even after loss.

New Opportunities Beyond Loss

One of the most surprising discoveries in this season of grief has been the way new opportunities have quietly emerged – not in spite of my loss, but because of what God has done through it. In the early days, I couldn't see past the sorrow. My future felt blank, like someone had taken a pen and drawn a hard line through the rest of the story. But over time, and often in the most unexpected ways, doors began to open. Conversations I never planned, invitations I never sought out, moments I never imagined – each one became a glimpse of something I thought had died with Cathy: Purpose.

These new opportunities didn't come all at once. They came slowly, gently – like spring buds after a long winter. At first, I wasn't even sure I was ready to step into them. But with each yes, each small act of obedience, I began to see that God was building something in the ashes of what I had lost. Not a replacement. Not a distraction. But a continuation – a new chapter that carried forward everything Cathy and I had built together, and everything God was still calling me to become. I didn't go looking for these opportunities. They found me as I chose to live forward. And with every new open door, I began to believe again – not only in the goodness of God, but in the possibility of purpose beyond loss.

Speaking on the Holy Spirit at My Granddaughter's High School

When my granddaughter asked me to speak at her high school chapel, I was incredibly honored. But when she told me the topic, she wanted me to speak on – the Holy Spirit – I felt something stir deep inside me. This wasn't just a chance to give a message. It was something sacred. It was a holy reminder that even in my grief, my family still saw me as a spiritual leader. They still trusted the voice of faith inside of me. That one invitation reminded me that even though Cathy was gone, my influence as a husband, father, and Papa was not.

I wasn't standing on a platform that day – I was standing on the gym floor of her high school, surrounded by students who were living through one of the most emotionally intense and pressure-filled seasons of life. I knew this moment wasn't about preaching a perfect sermon – it was about building a bridge. So, I started by trying to meet them where they were. I talked about the pressures they faced – grades, expectations, social comparisons, friendships, loneliness, and the constant influence of social media that can make it feel like everyone else's life is perfect while yours is falling apart. I told them, honestly, that I've faced those kinds of pressures too, just in different seasons and forms: We're all asking the same question: "Am I enough?"

Then I told them what I came to share – that the Holy Spirit is not some distant theological idea. He's a real and personal presence who helps us navigate life when it's too much to carry. The Holy Spirit doesn't just live in the pages of Scripture – He lives in us. He walks with us, speaks to us, strengthens us, and reminds us that we're never alone.

And then I shared something raw. I told them that eight months earlier, I had walked through the most painful and disorienting season of my life. I told them about Cathy – my high school sweetheart, the girl I met at 17, married at 18, and shared nearly 53 years together. How we had built a life, raised a family, served in ministry – and how one day, cancer came and changed everything. I told them that on June 28th, 2024, she passed away from a fierce battle with Stage 4 Ovarian Cancer.

I didn't hold back. I shared with them that the week after her death, I didn't even want to live. That I couldn't eat. Couldn't sleep. Couldn't pray. I told them I was confused. I didn't understand why God didn't answer my prayers for healing. I had believed. I had fasted. I had hoped. And yet … she was gone. But in that space – in the depths of pain, confusion, and silence – there was one constant: The Holy Spirit.

I told them that I couldn't explain it fully, but it felt like the Holy Spirit was hovering over me, holding me, whispering peace when everything inside me was screaming. He didn't take the pain away – but He never let me go. And now, looking back, I'm so thankful. Thankful for the peace that surpassed understanding. Thankful for the strength to keep breathing. Thankful for the hope that slowly returned. And I told them, "The same Holy Spirit who carried me through my deepest grief can carry you through your greatest challenges, too."

Before I closed, I shared how they could be filled with the Holy Spirit – not through striving or perfection, but through surrender. I told them He's not reserved for the super-spiritual. He's for the hurting, the honest, and the open. And I reminded them that life won't get easier as they grow older – but the presence of the Holy Spirit will make them stronger, wiser, and more anchored in truth. As I walked away from the podium, I was overwhelmed with gratitude – not just for the chance to speak but for the quiet assurance that God was still using my life, even in my pain. And I knew deep in my heart: the only reason I was able to stand there that day and speak about the goodness of God was because the Holy Spirit sustained me. Without His strength, I wouldn't have been able to do it. I had nothing left on my own – but He filled in every gap.

I'm sharing this moment in this chapter because it represents everything this season of my life has become. I'm no longer speaking from a place of ministry experience – I'm speaking from the place of loss, of healing, of rediscovered purpose. That morning in the high school gym wasn't just about teaching students about the Holy Spirit. It was about testifying to how real and present He has been in my journey through grief. It was one of the clearest moments I've seen where God took my brokenness and turned it into purpose. That's what this chapter is about. That's why I'm telling you this story.

Because even after loss God is not done. And the Holy Spirit – the same one who helped me breathe again, speak again, live again – is still writing new chapters through my life. And through yours, too. I never would have imagined that my first message after Cathy's death would be to a room full of high school students about the Holy Spirit. Back in 2022, when we first received Cathy's diagnosis, I never could have imagined where this journey would take me. But God did. And I'm so glad I said yes.

Leading Communion at Church

When my campus pastor, Lincoln, invited me to lead communion during our church's one-year anniversary celebration, it was another moment that confirmed something in my spirit. Even though I was still walking through the valley of grief, God was using my story in ways I never could have planned.

Communion is always sacred, but that day, it carried even more weight. Communion is about remembering – remembering Christ's sacrifice, His faithfulness, His presence. And as I stood before my church family, leading them through this holy act, I wasn't just helping them remember what Jesus did – I was remembering how His presence had sustained me through grief.

But there was more. As I looked around that room, I was overwhelmed with gratitude. Just a year earlier, Cathy had sat with me in that same building, celebrating its opening. It was the fulfillment of a long-held vision – something we had prayed for, sacrificed for, and believed for together. She got to see it. God, in His mercy, allowed her to see the fruit of her faith before He called her home. And that day, as I held the bread and the cup, I gave thanks – not just for Christ's sacrifice, but for the quiet kindness of God who let my wife witness the goodness of His promise before her passing.

In that moment, I sensed something deep and clear: God is not finished with me. There's still work to do. There's still a purpose to fulfill. Leading communion wasn't just an honor – it was a reminder. A reminder that even in loss, life can be deeply meaningful. That grief doesn't disqualify you from being used by God – it often deepens your capacity to serve with compassion and humility. And as I spoke words of remembrance and hope, I also whispered a silent prayer of gratitude: *Thank You, Lord, for letting Cathy see the fruit of her faith. And thank you for letting me carry it forward.*

The Impact of Grieving Well on Others

Grieving well isn't just about me – it's about people around me who are watching my journey. What I've come to realize is that how I live in the wake of loss doesn't happen in a vacuum. People are paying attention. My kids. My grandkids. My neighbors. My church. Even people I barely know. In quiet moments, in everyday interactions, they've seen me walk through grief not with perfection, but with honest faith. And in doing so, they've found strength for their own struggles.

One of the most unexpected and meaningful moments came from my neighbors, Cole and Chelsey – brand-new Christians. They've told me more than once how watching me grieve has had a deep impact on them. Not because I had the right words, but because they saw how I carried myself in the hard days. They didn't just see my grief – they saw my faith in action. They saw that I didn't collapse under the weight of loss, and that my hope wasn't pretend. It was real. And that reality made them hungry to grow in their own faith.

They've said to me, "We're watching how you walk through this." And I'll never forget that. It reminded me that our grief becomes a living testimony. The way we trust God when everything in us wants to pull away ... the way we show up even when our heart is still healing ... the way we speak hope even when tears are close to the surface – all of that preaches louder than any sermon. People need to see that it's possible to grieve deeply and still live fully. And that's what I want my life to reflect.

Grieving Well to Live Well

What I've learned is this: Grieving well is what allows me to live well. I'm not moving forward because the pain is gone. I'm moving forward because I've surrendered the pain to God and said, "Use it." I'm not living with purpose for myself alone. I'm doing it for my family. For my community. For the people God keeps placing in my path. I want to live in a way that honors Cathy's legacy, reflects God's goodness, and inspires others to keep going.

Grief doesn't just disappear one day – it becomes a part of the story. And how we carry that story says something. The way we carry grief becomes a testimony. It either shows people that loss is the end, or that it can be the beginning of something meaningful and redemptive. When people look at my life now, I hope they don't just see a man who lost his wife. I hope they see a man who still believes. A man who is still walking. A man who is still listening for the voice of God and saying yes when He speaks.

People don't just hear our words – they watch our lives. They notice how we respond to heartbreak, how we treat others, how we carry sorrow and hope at the same time. And that speaks louder than anything I could ever say. To grieve well is to live well. And to live well after loss is one of the most powerful testimonies we can offer this world. Not because we're strong – but because God is strong in us.

Investing in the Next Generation

If there's one thing I've learned in this season of life, it's this: Our purpose isn't tied to a single role or moment in time – it's found in the people we pour into. And for me, that has never been clearer than in the time I spend with my grandchildren. Whether it's grabbing a casual lunch, going to a play, or simply showing up for one of their events, I've come to see these moments as sacred. They're not just family outings – they're opportunities to stay present, to speak into their lives, and to build something lasting. Purpose didn't end when Cathy passed – it widened. It took on new meaning in the lives of those who carry our legacy forward.

Some of my most meaningful moments have come through simple conversations – sitting across from one of my grandkids at a restaurant, listening to their hopes, their doubts, their questions about life and faith. It's in those unhurried moments that I realize how vital it is to be available. To not just love them but to guide them. And I don't take that lightly. Every meal, every text, every request for prayer is a reminder that my influence still matters – that even though I've walked through loss, God is still using my voice to shape hearts.

Several of my grandchildren are involved in Youth With A Mission (YWAM), boldly traveling the world to share the gospel. I've watched with pride and awe as they step into places and situations I never imagined at their age – full of courage and faith. And what humbles me most is that they still want me involved. They reach out, not just to share updates, but to ask for wisdom, to seek prayer, to process what they're seeing and doing. These aren't just surface-level conversations. They're evidence that the investment we make in the next generation doesn't expire with age or sorrow – it grows deeper. I may not be on the mission field with them, but through encouragement, prayer, and presence, I'm walking alongside them – cheering them on, pointing them to Jesus, and staying faithful in my role as their Papa.

As I've continued walking this road of grief and growth, one word keeps rising to the surface – one word that seems to frame everything I've experienced this season …

The Word That Defines My Life: Purpose

If there's one word that has surfaced more than any other during this chapter of life, it's purpose. But it didn't arrive with clarity or confidence.

It came quietly, like a question I didn't know how to answer. After Cathy passed, I wasn't looking for purpose – I was just trying to make sense of the silence. The routines we once shared were gone, the future we had imagined had vanished. For a while, I wondered if my most meaningful days were behind me.

But purpose has a way of finding you when you're not chasing it. It started to show up in small ways – through people reaching out, through conversations I didn't expect to have, through moments of honest connection. It wasn't about stepping into something big. It was about staying available. And slowly, I began to see that meaning isn't something we find after the pain – it's something God threads through it.

These days, purpose looks different than it did before. It's not about busyness or building something new. It's about being present and faithful with what's right in front of me. A conversation with a grandchild. A note of encouragement to someone hurting. A quiet moment of prayer for someone who feels lost. It's not flashy, but it's deeply fulfilling. My life may look simpler on the outside, but it feels richer on the inside – because I know that even now, there's still impact to be made.

That's what purpose means to me in this season: Living with open hands and a soft heart, trusting that even the smallest steps of obedience still matter in the hands of God.

Encouragement for Those Seeking Purpose After Loss

I know I've said this before, but it bears repeating – because I know someone needs to hear it again: If you're in the early stages of grief and you feel like you'll never have purpose again, I understand. I've been there. I know what it's like to wake up with the ache still fresh, to look ahead and see nothing but emptiness where your future used to be. I truly believed my best days were behind me. The idea of doing anything meaningful again felt far away – maybe even impossible.

But here's what I've learned: purpose doesn't end with loss. It may feel buried for a while, and it might take time to uncover, but it doesn't disappear. In fact, I've come to believe that when we allow God to meet us in our grief – when we invite Him to walk with us through the pain – purpose doesn't just return, it deepens. Loss expands our capacity to feel, to notice others, to love more intentionally. It may not be the purpose we once imagined, but it's real. And it matters.

Maybe right now you don't feel ready. Maybe just getting through the day is all you can manage. Maybe the idea of serving or leading or pouring into someone else feels way too soon. And you know what? That's okay. Healing takes time. God is not in a hurry. He's not waiting for you to *get over it* – He's walking with you through it. But when the time comes – and it will – you'll begin to sense that quiet invitation to step forward. You'll feel the nudge to share, to connect, to care. Sometimes in big ways – like speaking to a group, mentoring someone, or leading something meaningful. But more often, it comes in the small, sacred moments. A conversation that matters. A text that brings comfort. A listening ear when someone else is hurting.

Purpose doesn't have to be loud to be life-changing. Often, it begins in the quiet spaces where grief has softened our hearts and opened us to God in a new way. You may feel like your life has been put on pause – but it hasn't. Your story is still unfolding. God isn't done with you. Even in your grief – *especially* in your grief – He is calling you to live again. Not just to survive, but to live with intention, to love deeply, and to serve from a place of compassion and truth.

And here's what I've discovered along the way: When you begin to live that way, even with a broken heart, you will find something you never expected – joy in the midst of sorrow, meaning that grows out of pain, and purpose that runs deeper than you ever knew. This isn't the life you planned, but it can still be full of goodness, beauty, and impact. You are not forgotten. You are not finished. And God still has something beautiful for your life.

Writing This Book - A Purpose I Never Saw Coming

If you had asked me a year ago whether I'd ever write a book – especially one about grief – I would have gently laughed and told you no. I didn't have a message, only a broken heart. I wasn't trying to teach or lead anyone through pain. I was just trying to survive my own. The weight of losing Cathy was all-consuming. Every day felt like a mountain to climb. The last thing on my mind was writing. And yet, somewhere along the way, a quiet change began to take root. What began as journaling, as reflection, as prayer, slowly became a calling I hadn't expected.

At first, I wasn't sure what I was doing. I just knew that if my story could help even one person feel less alone, if it could remind someone that hope was still possible, then maybe – just maybe – God could use it.

The more I wrote, the more I realized this wasn't just about my grief. It was about our shared humanity, our need for comfort, for truth, and for the assurance that God meets us in the hardest places of life. Writing this book became not just a project – it became part of my healing.

There were moments I had to pause because the memories were too fresh. Other times, I found tears falling onto the keyboard as I relived the sacred and painful parts of our journey. But every time I felt like stopping, I sensed God reminding me: *This matters. Keep going.* What I thought would be a quiet reflection has become one of the greatest purposes to rise from my pain. This book is a part of Cathy's legacy – and mine, too.

Through these pages, I've learned that purpose doesn't always shout. Sometimes it whispers in the stillness. Sometimes it arrives unexpectedly, hidden inside sorrow, waiting to be uncovered through obedience. I never set out to write a book. But God, in His mercy, gave me this gift – not just to share with others, but to remind me that He's still writing my story, too.

I hope these words reach the hearts they're meant to reach. I hope someone who feels like their life is over picks up this book and begins to believe that they're not alone, and they're not done. I hope someone who has loved deeply and lost deeply finds comfort, companionship, and courage on these pages. Most of all, I hope they see Jesus here – not just in the hope beyond the grave, but in the purpose that still lives on this side of it.

Study Guide

Bible Study Helps: Reflect and Apply

Chapter Nine Summary: This chapter explores the beauty and depth of living with purpose after profound loss. It's not about rushing past grief – it's about opening your heart to what God still wants to do in and through your life. Purpose might look different now, but it's no less meaningful. Whether through serving others, investing in family, saying yes to new opportunities, or even writing a book, your story matters. God is not finished with you.

Key Scriptures for Reflection

Philippians 1:6	*"He who has begun a good work in you will complete it until the day of Jesus Christ."*
Romans 8:28	*"And we know that all things work together for good to those who love God, to those who are the called according to His purpose."*
2 Corinthians 1:3–4	*"…the God of all comfort, who comforts us in all our tribulation, that we may be able to comfort those who are in any trouble…"*
Isaiah 61:3	*"To console those who mourn in Zion, to give them beauty for ashes, the oil of joy for mourning."*
Psalm 138:8	*"The* LORD *will fulfill His purpose for me; your steadfast love, O* LORD, *endures forever …"* (ESV).

Reflection Questions

1. Do you believe your life still has purpose, even in this season of grief? Why or why not?
2. What moments – big or small – have helped you rediscover meaning after your loss?

3. Have you ever felt God calling you to something that scared you or felt too soon? How did you respond?
4. What role does your story play in encouraging others who are grieving?
5. How can you begin investing in others – even in quiet, simple ways – right where you are?

Going Deeper

Think about how your unique story might offer encouragement, comfort, or perspective to someone else. Purpose doesn't always arrive through platforms or big assignments. Sometimes it's found in a single conversation, a quiet act of faithfulness, or an unexpected opportunity to show up. Ask the Lord to show you one person this week who may need a reminder that their story isn't over – and be willing to speak life into them.

Prayer Prompt

Lord, I admit there have been moments when I didn't think my life still had purpose. The pain felt too heavy, and the future felt uncertain. But I believe You are still working in me and through me. Help me to say yes when You call. Help me to trust that my story still matters. And give me the courage to live well, love deeply, and serve others – even in my sorrow. Thank You that You're not done with me yet. Amen. *(Use the space on the next page to write your prayer.)*

_____

_____

_____

_____

_____

_____

_____

Journal Your Thoughts

_____

_____

_____

_____

_____

_____

_____

_____

_____

_____

_____

_____

CHAPTER 10

A Final Encouragement

IF YOU'RE READING THIS, it means you have walked through this journey with me. And that means something profound: You've found the courage to face your grief head-on. You've wrestled with pain, searched for hope, and opened your heart to healing – even when it felt impossible.

Maybe you have lost someone you love, and you've been searching for answers. Maybe you've been wondering if life will ever be full again … if joy is still possible … if there is truly hope beyond grief.

I want to tell you - yes, there is!

Not because grief disappears. Not because life will ever be exactly the same again. But because grieving well leads to living well.

At the beginning of this journey, I couldn't imagine a life where hope and happiness could exist alongside the weight of loss. But I have learned that hope doesn't erase grief – hope carries you through it.

Your grief is not weakness - it's testimony.

I don't know your story. I don't know who you've lost, how deeply you've loved, or how heavy your pain feels today. But I do know this – your grief is a testimony to love. We grieve deeply because we have loved deeply. And because that love was real, the loss is real. But so is the hope that follows.

If you take anything away from this book, let it be this: You are still here. That means your story is not over. That means there is still love to give, life to live, and purpose to walk into. You are not dishonoring your loved one by choosing to live again. In fact, living well is one of the greatest ways to honor them.

It's okay to keep moving forward.

Moving forward does not mean forgetting. It does not mean leaving behind the love you shared. Moving forward simply means choosing to keep living – not just surviving but truly living. That might mean saying yes to new friendships. It might mean opening your heart again, even when it feels vulnerable. It might mean discovering passions and purpose you never expected.

For me, it meant trusting that God was not finished with my story. It meant letting my family love me, letting my faith sustain me, and saying yes when opportunities came – opportunities I never thought I'd have again. And it has meant reminding myself, every single day, that I can carry hope and grief at the same time.

And so can you.

A Personal Challenge to You

As you close this book, I want to challenge you. Not in a heavy or overwhelming way, but in a way that gently calls you forward.

- Find one thing today that reminds you life is still good.
- Say yes to something that brings you joy, even if it feels unfamiliar.
- Let yourself imagine a future filled with meaning and purpose.

You don't have to have it all figured out. Just take one step. Then another. And another. God is not finished with your story. There is still beauty to witness, still joy to experience, still love to give. There is hope beyond this moment – and it's waiting for you.

Keep walking – you will find it!

A Personal Note from the Author

IF YOU'VE MADE IT THIS FAR, I WANT TO THANK YOU – not just for reading my story, but for allowing me to walk with you through your own journey of grief. Writing this book was never about having all the answers – it was about being honest in the struggle, in the pain, and in the hope that follows.

I don't know what loss you've experienced. I don't know what empty chair you're staring at, what memories make your heart ache, or what questions keep you up at night. But I do know this – you are not alone.

Grief is one of the hardest roads you will ever walk. It doesn't come with a clear map, and it certainly doesn't come with easy answers. Some days will feel unbearable. Some moments will take your breath away, not because of joy, but because of the weight of what's missing. And yet, somehow, step by step, you will move forward. Not away from your love. Not away from the person you lost. But toward a new way of carrying them with you.

That's what it means to grieve well.

It's not about *moving on* or pretending the pain isn't real. It's about honoring the life you had with them by choosing to keep living your own. It's about finding hope in the middle of sorrow, strength in the middle of weakness, and purpose when everything feels shattered.

I didn't think I could find purpose again. I thought my life ended when Cathy's did. But I can tell you now – there is life beyond loss.

There is joy beyond sorrow. There is hope beyond the horizon.

And if I can find it, so can you.

So, wherever you are today, whether you are in the depths of fresh grief or slowly making your way toward healing, I want to leave you with this: Your story isn't over. You have more life to live, more love to give, and more purpose than you can imagine. Take your time. Give yourself grace. And when you're ready – take the next step forward.

Grieve well. Live well. And never forget – hope is waiting for you.

I'd love to hear your story!

If you've walked through loss, found hope in the midst of pain, or are still somewhere in between, I'd be honored to hear from you. And if this book has encouraged you or helped you in any way, I'd be grateful to know that as well.

Please feel free to email me at: davemcbroom@comcast.net. I read every message and count it a privilege to listen to how God is meeting people in their sorrow and gently writing new chapters of healing and purpose.

With love and understanding,

Dave McBroom

Bibliography

Dunn, Bill and Kathy Leonard. *Through a Season of Grief: 365 Devotions for Your Journey from Mourning to Joy.* Thomas Nelson, 2021.

Lewis, C.S. *A Grief Observed*. HarperOne, 2015. (Originally published under the pseudonym N.W. Clerk. Farber and Farber, 1961.)

Roe, Gary. *Comfort For the Grieving Spouse's Heart: Hope and Healing After Losing Your Partner.* Gary Roe, 2019.

Zonnebelt-Smeenge, Susan and Robert C. DeVries. *Getting to the Other Side of Grief: Overcoming the Loss of a Spouse.* Baker House, 2019.

www.ingramcontent.com/pod-product-compliance
Lightning Source LLC
Chambersburg PA
CBHW051626120626
46551CB00014B/1954